Deceptions, Distractions & Disillusionment: Barriers to Your Success and Ours

By Michael A. Wright, PhD

mawmedia
Group

Nashville TN

Publisher: MAWMedia Group

© 2016 by Michael A. Wright (michael@mawmedia.com).

First Edition: February 2016

Deceptions, Distractions & Disillusionment: Barriers to Your Success and Ours/ By Michael A. Wright, PhD

ISBN: 978-1-943616-12-1

MAWMedia Group, LLC
2525 Somerset Drive
Nashville, TN 37217

www.mawmedia.com

Cover graphic "Gala Apple On White Background" courtesy of Feelart from freedigitalphotos.net

DEDICATION

To my grandmother: You always spoke with wisdom, encouragement, and certainty. You taught me to pursue happiness without hesitation, seek truth without fainting, and live without regret. Thank you, grandma.

PROLOGUE

Revelation: It's not about you, but it is your responsibility

The meaning of life is not a simple answer to your individual existence, but it is a function of your choice to act responsibly. I know that my best self will only be achieved in concert with you being your best self. And therein lies the challenge to our collective vision of perfection. I am not fearful of those that challenge me. I am not perplexed by those that conspire against me. I am not deterred by those that stand in my way. I am concerned with you who, for whatever reason, have not practiced your gifts or developed your talents. Now, I stand ready with my part of our collective vision, and you are not ready with your contribution. And, to add insult, you stand almost proud to proclaim that you have no clue of your gift and talents—no knowledge of the context of the choice you are responsible for.

Once, it was my fault as well as yours. Let me first apologize to those who came prepared before me. I apologize. I let many of you down. But, I learned. I have since been ready with my contribution at every opportunity. I have been called arrogant, conceited, know-it-all, and the like, but my detractors could not compete with the sound nature of my counsel. They could never question my preparation. I have been cast out of some circles, and self-exited from others. But, I have become unique, some may say peculiar. I now call to you to leave the comfort of conformity and renew your mind.

My call to you comes with an explanation. I am certain that it will be difficult to challenge your prevailing beliefs about your ability to influence the way the world works. I cannot promise that you will, in fact, achieve nirvana. But, I can with certainty educate you to define your role in society, offer a relationship based on reciprocity, and walk with you confidently to access new markets. To achieve these goals, we first must address your waste of mental energies. I chose the cognitive restructuring method in order to model for you how the very definitions you stand with today must give way to a vocabulary of a certain successful future.

Rather than focus on personifications of an enemy such as a Satan, or your boss, or the parent who failed you, this discourse refocuses the analysis on you. Admittedly, it is a more abstract proposition, but the barrier, the waste of energy itself is the enemy. We will thoroughly identify your dependence on the enemy for your own subsistence. Then, I will offer an alternative—a newly defined role, an approach to lifelong learning from diverse sources, and a system of continued productivity.

Next time I need you and your contribution, I would like for you to be ready. The deceptions, distractions, and disillusionment that keep you inactive and unresponsive to my invitation must give way to productive action toward our collective vision. My success is mine to achieve. My excellence is a given. My perfection depends on you.

Fallacy: Community's Function is to Determine Truth

If you wanted to conquer the world, the method would be simple, yet brilliant: change the basic definitions of community. Utilize a behavioral intervention to perpetrate a mass hysteria with the goal of creating dissociative mental states as the norm. Utilize the need for homeostasis in each individual (and the penchant for laziness) and create institutions that force the balance of reason and emotion into unhealthy, irresponsible, poorly informed, yet comfortable choices. Seat the fallacy in institutions, because humans typically do not question the institution—the proverbial "they." Create a sense and sensitivity to scarcity. Construct relationships as zero-sum propositions, in which each party must give an equal share to add up to an ever-diminishing one hundred percent. Withdrawals of 25% leave 75% for others. When the coffers are fully withdrawn, those who have nothing are without option.

Under the guise faith, convince a generation that blind belief without question ensures that "rightness" is preserved as a bulwark against loss, pain, and distress. Support that generation to teach their children a need for rightness as an action rather than rightness as an identity of justice. Define "right" as "truth," "truth" as immutable, and immutability as strength of faith. Subtly, remove the greatest power from each individual: choice—the choice to challenge, the choice to question, and the choice to be great. Reduce a once empowering choice to a sophomoric question of in-group versus outsider—a question of a desire to belong.

Humans want relationship. We want to belong to something greater than our individual selves. And, often, we do not care what the cost is.

The institution has provided comfort that you can see. Others have conformed and prospered. You join with the others in **our new blind faith**, without question, with no request for reciprocity. Together, you build the strength of your immutable truth. You know

10

it is the truth—the ultimate level of our development potential—because it is not the "evil" you were participating in before. This is the fallacy of diminishing community to nothing more than a faceless, ritualistic, exclusive in-group. It's an US thing, THEY wouldn't understand.

Explanation: The Fallacy in Psychological Terms

The above simplifies some complex human psychology and sociology. Basically, your dissonance with your social role has been rectified by assuming a *group identity* instead of working to create consonance with a clearly defined *individual identity*. This allows you the luxury of aggregate success—you are a success because you belong to a successful corporate body. But, this is not success grounded in living up to your full potential. It is ultimately hollow in the face of hardships because the individual parts are not strong enough to endure. If you are ever to really succeed, you must redefine your role, continue to gain information from multiple sources, and endure the disappointment of inconsistencies by actively testing the fit of new information with your personal goals.

I submit that your unsustainable responses to your dissonance—your attempt to regain balance and comfort—can take three forms: deception, distraction, or disillusionment. Each of the forms describes a state of mind suggested by your environmental inputs and affecting your choice behavior. Deception suggests a set of information that is error-laden and incomplete. You have no means to make informed choices, and your lack of information keeps you from insisting on better data. Deceived, your choices appear more limited than they are in reality. Distraction keeps valuable information away from you by focusing your attention on other things, often irrelevant things. You argue and protest, but the allowance you seek is a trifle, an insignificant victory when compared against your just reward.

Disillusionment paints you into a corner of powerlessness and helplessness. You remove yourself from considering the choices available. You are told that you do not have the authority to determine your role and make choices. Disillusionment states that you have not grown into it or earned your role.

Your single most important strength is your power to make a choice. Until now, your choices have lacked a defined role, have been misinformed, and have been made for speed and convenience rather than sustainability. It is now time to invest in the real you. Define your individual passion--your role. Learn and continue to seek information from diverse sources. Endure productively the process of time. Succeed!

The Challenge: Your Identity is tied to the Fallacy

The challenge is that you do not believe me. You have been brainwashed. The fallacy of community as in-group is so much a part of how you construct your sense of self that my proposition threatens your core identity. As a matter of self-protection, you resist this new information. An easy indicator is your insistence on relegating every relationship to a "family" relationship. At work, you are part of a family. Your treatment group has become a family to you. Your weekly spin class is more than exercise, it has become a family. This in-group preoccupation allows you to hide in a familiar role, behind the hem and protection of your benevolent "parents:" the bosses, the group leaders, the administrators. You have the luxury of complaining about their rules and limitations never being challenged to come up with your own. In the context of the family analogy, you never move out of your comfortable home to create and be responsible for your own family.

Through this text, I present an exercise that offers a beginning to your cognitive restructuring. I hope you will re-educate yourself.

Move beyond what you have been told to seek new information. I hope you will find a balance in productivity that contributes to our vision. I hope you will reclaim your power to create.

Recognize that this text is not a call to make me a king, to credit me with your re-education and reclamation, or to call you to another in-group. It is a call for non-dual existence—both, and. Granted, it is not about you, but it is your responsibility. It is completely up to you, but the benefit reaches beyond the limitations of your understanding. It is your choice ultimately to live in the spirit of the power you were granted in the beginning. It is your responsibility to take your rightful place, to get the information first-hand, to stay in the race and endure. To succeed, you must be able to define roles for yourself, determine truth for yourself, and encourage yourself. This text will point out bread crumbs. It is up to you to choose the path.

The single challenge of life is **choice** to manage your desire for purpose and order, summed up in 3 statements:

1. FORGIVENESS: I take responsibility for my choices to seek knowledge, define my social role, and engage in relationships. I approach every interaction as productive. With each choice, I am leaving a legacy that endures with sustainability to my children's children.
2. PERFECTION: I determine my path. I am a captain with permission, perspective, and purpose. Without apology, I own my desires. I benefit from new information. I act with intention.
3. AGENCY: I make choices in a way that encourages responsibility and inspires leadership in others. I develop leaders from followers to achieve beyond what I have achieved. I celebrate progress as success. I learn from every outcome.

You have been systematically miseducated such that these words (forgiveness, perfection, and agency) are understood to be a burden of unreachable expectations. I will first open your eyes to the deceptions, distractions, and disillusionment that have served to miseducate you. We will then redefine these words and support your success knowing that you can gain peace, you can live in excellence, and you can inspire others by being your best, unapologetically!

Deceptions: You don't know yourself, and you don't develop. You deceive yourself into thinking you are developing because you are doing something—the same thing with no results. At its core, all you are doing is defending against your perceptions of yourself as inferior, unworthy, and incapable.

Distractions: You focus on a method of success that is not your own seeking to compete with the same tools others have used. The focus is on gaining power, prestige, and status rather than gaining relationships, exhorting others, and contributing to community.

Disillusionment: You accept the pattern of your failure and take yourself out of the game waiting for a breakthrough without being active and intentional in the markets, distracted by a limited comprehension of the options available and a diminished understanding of the power and authority you represent.

SECTION I: DECEPTIONS

Deceptions: Incomplete or erroneous information about you and the environment.

CHAPTER 1
DECEPTIONS: BARRIERS TO ROLE DEFINITION

"Now the serpent was more subtle than any beast of the field which the Lord God had made..." Genesis 3:1.

Deception occurs when you possess no identifiable baseline for your social role. Your assessment of progress does not include an assessment of self-development in addition to learning. The result is that you are not motivated to challenge yourself to learn, and you do not change your behavior to bring congruence between the person you are (habits) and what you want to achieve (goals).

Learning, Development & the Wisdom of Reason

That feeling that your beliefs contain some logical fallacies is called dissonance. Dissonance precipitates action. Learning can be defined as your attempt to handle feelings of dissonance. Self-development is the result of utilizing learning to redefine your role and increase your information by quantity and sources. You can learn without developing, but you cannot develop without learning.

You certainly have been faced with situations that cause stress. When this stress causes you to question beliefs about yourself and your values it is called *dissonance*. In dissonant situations, you seek to find more information about the stressor in order to return to your previous, lower stress state. Learning is a way to deal with dissonance. In this way, **learning** is defined as knowledge acquisition to alleviate anxiety or stress.

Consonance is the opposite of dissonance. The desire for consonance motivates the creation of a structured worldview. That is, you learn to view the world and your place within it in ways that reduce your stress. But, this role definition causes stress in itself. Often, your carefully constructed understanding of the world is not sufficient to alleviate stress or explain the tragedies of the world.

The relationship between stress through dissonance and learning may be why some people think that suffering is a requirement for learning valuable life lessons. The stress of suffering can create opportunity and motivation for learning. Yet, true learning results in behavior change through a process of conditioning. This is as opposed to a knee-jerk reaction to rid yourself of stress. True learning is characterized by autonomy, license, and tangible products. Two issues present here:

1) Stress does not always result in sustainable behavior change. Sometimes it causes you to run and hide.
2) Learning at its best is entered into willingly so that an awareness of the knowledge in context aligns with motivation to produce transferrable skills.

Because of this, you choose one of two basic options: learn more or refuse to believe evidence. If you choose to learn more, you have to find a social environment that will inform you. If you chose to refuse to believe, you have to find some social environment in which to shield yourself from opposing views. This is the great deception. It threatens to destroy your opportunity for self-development based in the realization that your learning is insufficient.

You find social environments that attend to your presenting need for information with a calming, safe, reaffirming worldview rather than the exploration of dissonance and its challenges and questions. Your goal is only to alleviate the stress, not to resolve the dissonance. Through the safe havens, you can feel validated in your previous knowledge, confident that you have learned because you reacted to the dissonance. You exhibit no negatively reinforcing behaviors, and the choice was yours autonomously.

The problem is that you did not lose anything. You participated in a closed-system loop. Input your worldview. Output your worldview. If you experienced stress in the context of a worldview you held, that worldview cannot be simply reaffirmed. It must be updated to explain the dissonance. This updating of your worldview can be termed development. Development requires a loosening of your structured worldview. **Self-development** is the process of redefining your role in the context of the worldview that you perceive. Wisdom is the result of reflective, open-system determination of the best way to use knowledge. **Wisdom** is the combination of both learning and self-development. Wisdom requires you to see the world in an informed way and define your place within the world.

Simple behaviorism (to be distinguished from radical behaviorism or learning theory, which incorporates cognitive realms) views the process of social role definition as a natural process of automatic and conditioned responses. Much like simple learning without development, behaviorism proffers that the response to stress is an attempt to return to equilibrium and low-stress. You have the capacity, as a human animal, to exercise autonomy within a social context. That is, learning can be combined with self-development as an experience beyond the search for reduced stress. You can build a view of the world that is fluid, and activate the power within yourself to define a specific role. You can create tangible products to influence the world around you.

Beyond Behaviorist Learning

More than a simple function of automatic and conditioned responses, human behavior is steeped in how you define your role in the world and how you interact within your community. In other words, you behave in ways that fit with the way you see yourself. You update this view of self in response to interactions with other people. Change in response to interactions or recognized fallacies in your worldview or inconsistencies in your behavior can be productive as you are reflective and open to new information. Inhibiting this productivity is the fact that humans are more comfortable with stable views of the world and stable views of themselves. The preference for stability may lead to limits in the process of role redefinition and limits in the variety of interactions you experience. When new information is limited in this way, you can maintain a stable, reassuring view of yourself and the world around you.

A constant state of chaos is not advisable. As well, considering a change in belief or behavior is no obligation to change. But, when you find that your sense of self and your behaviors are inconsistent, it may be time to map the inconsistency and consider change. What typically occurs though is a redoubling of our protectionist instincts. Redirection, counterfeiting, and rationalization are comfortable processes we use to regain equilibrium without considering change.

Notice that each of the following is a mechanism you use to maintain safety and stability. The human tendency toward self-protection makes your struggle even more daunting. Risk is uncomfortable, but it is necessary.

Redirection: Defining Your Role

Redirection enables what psychologists call fixed action patterns. Fixed action patterns are better known as habits. Some of the habits you practice inhibit your continued learning and self-development. These habits are especially damaging when they are prescribed by institutional bylaws, doctrines, or creeds, which do not change easily. Redirection reinforces your habits while obscuring the reality that your desired future is not being achieved. You begin to see the pattern as productive because you can count on it—not for future success, but for present stability.

Correcting redirection as a protectionist instinct begins with attention to the power and potential of your gifts—to match your view of yourself with a definition of your future success. Defining your future success requires that you take responsibility for your future. You must stop giving in to the temptation to lean on institutions or stable patterns that obscure the fact that you are no closer to your goals than when you began the habit. Risk is part of the process, not suffering. There is no need to fear the suffering. You will sweat and sacrifice, but your effort must yield results.

At its core, redirection is a choice of worldview, specifically perception of the future. At its worse, the question of success is defined as a question of comfort and stability—a definition that does not motivate changes, and therefore, ensures failure. Redirection encapsulates a number of choices you must face in perception of your future and definition of your social role including: to invest or to buy, to energize or to drain energy, to lead or to manage, to captain or to navigate.

Counterfeiting: Defining Your Community

Counterfeiting refers to the mis-classification of your experiences. More than a mask you put on to deceive the world around you, counterfeiting is deception of yourself. You begin to define peak experiences in terms that lack the power and enduring quality of the genuine peak experience. You train yourself to be contented with an inferior quality of life that, in time, ceases to motivate you. Worse yet, I gain no motivation from your experience. You accept mediocrity as excellence. Depth of insight, genuineness of relationship, clarity of role is judged by how well it fits with your current understanding rather than the height of standard it calls you to obtain.

You begin to mistake counterfeited behavior as acceptable. You begin to display counterfeit behaviors because they look and feel positively reinforcing. But, often the short duration of your reinforcement and the lack of sustainability reveal that, in the long run, the behavior and relationships created on the basis of the counterfeit do not result in achievement of your goals.

The key to genuine interaction is to risk what you have come to protect: your feelings. You must speak your truth without placing a concern for the feelings of others above that truth. At the same time, you must allow others to hold their truth even in disagreement with yours. The mechanism is to live within the seeming contradiction of valuing others and their opinions and living decisively as a captain. Knowing the difference between counterfeit and the genuine is to cultivate diverse sources of information. The potential harm of being wrong decreases with the amount of knowledge considered in the deliberation of a decision. And, in the end, the choice is yours to make and to live with...and to celebrate. No matter the outcome, you acted genuinely representing and admonishing an atmosphere of genuineness.

Rationalization: Learning Without Development

Rationalization refers to your tendency to explain unsustainable choices. Rather than examining both your beliefs about a situation and the behaviors involved, rationalization supports a possible change in behavior without any question of the underlying logic of the behavior and without any question of the social role you have defined for yourself. In many cases, rationalization functions to delay changes in your behavior.

I understand that your powers of reason are well-practiced. In fact, I recognize it as an indication of your potential for greatness. You must entertain all options, though, including the option that the depth of your error extends beyond the current choice and outcome. Your error is in your core definition of your social role. In other words, it is not just the "what you know" that you have opportunity to inform, it is also the "who are you" that needs to be redefined. It is a questioning of thoughts and feelings, knowledge and attitudes, learning and self-development.

I understand that this questioning is often difficult because the patterns of rationalization you employ have been passed down to you by people that you respect and revere: parents, pastors, mentors, and other loved ones. All knowledge must support the search for new knowledge and the potential for change (cognitive flexibility), or it is dogma and does not fit the definition of self-development. Once-for-all knowledge traps you in a mental prison and a developmental rut.

Recognize that it is not my intention to change your mind. My intention is to free your mind—to get you to start making choices for yourself. In order to be free, you need to recognize error when you encounter it. Much of this error has been your pattern, and it has served you well in your mind. Challenge yourself to reach beyond what has been easy up to this point. Systematically inspect the methods you have practiced to deceive yourself. Let's explore each deception in turn: Redirection, Counterfeiting, and Rationalization.

CHAPTER 2 REDIRECTION

"...and he said unto the woman, Yea hath God said, you shall not eat of every tree of the garden?" Genesis 3:1

Redirection occurs when you define success as role stability rather than role development.

Deceptions Case Study: 1 of 3

A story is told in an ancient text about a god who created the first humans. The man, the creator named Adam. Adam named the woman Eve. The creator created these beings with the same capacity as he held—the capacity to create. The creator placed Adam and Eve in a lush garden and instructed the man and woman that they were free to eat of every tree except one.

One day, Eve was walking near the forbidden tree. A voice from the tree engaged her. The voice asked, "The god told you that you could not eat from every tree?" And there, right there, he had her redirected. The deception was a subtle confusion. The creator was not oppressing Adam and Eve with his first instructions. The creator was freeing them. He did not begin with "you cannot." He began with "you are free." The issue under investigation was not the monotony of the menu and the prohibition. The important issue was how the prescribed menu freed Adam and Eve to focus on their relationship rather than worrying about food, shelter, and belonging.

This story of redirection is a cautionary tale for you. It is now time to focus on what you CAN do rather than being redirected to dwell on what you CANNOT do. When I come to you looking to collaborate, I am not interested in what you have not learned or are incapable of. I first want to know how you are able to partner with me—what you can add to our partnership. The sooner you recognize the gifts you have, the sooner you can begin to feed those gifts. Eve should have been using the food she had to fuel higher developmental needs. You should be confident with what you now know and have capacity to do. Now, focus on higher developmental needs. Let us connect in partnership.

If You Only Knew for Sure

Abraham Maslow created what he called a hierarchy of needs in 1943. The hierarchy orders what humans need to lead productive lives. From another perspective, it lists the prerequisites for self-transcendence. In Maslow's hierarchy, stable physiological needs enable safety and security. Safety enables love and belonging. Love enables esteem. Esteem enables self-actualization. Self-actualization enables self-transcendence.

Physiological is to Eat, Sleep, and Excrete. Safety is to touch and know for certain. Love is to find comfort in the knowing. Esteem is to find agency in the knowing. Self-actualization is to create new knowledge. Self-transcendence is to collaborate in new ways.

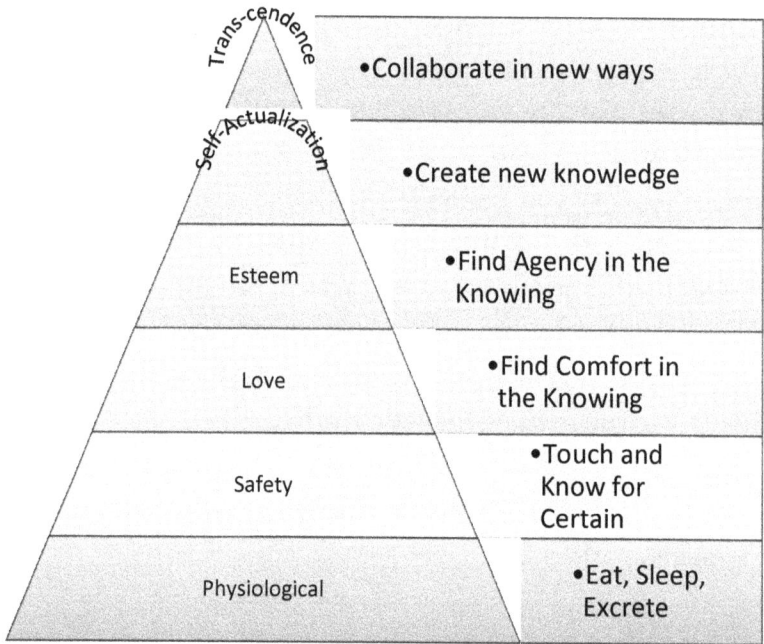

Physiology, Safety, Love, and Esteem are *deficit needs*. Deficit needs must be addressed and fulfilled before you can experience the *being needs* of self-actualization and self-transcendence. Physiology places importance on physical health and the proper function of the body. Safety and security explores the certainty with which you approach the world. Love and belonging moves beyond the simple physical and mental operations to the meaning and relationships you derive from interactions with others. Esteem extends the concepts of certainty and meaning allowing you to formulate self-confidence and the ability to team together with others.

You require therapeutic intervention, discipline, and a great deal of introspection in order to overcome the trauma, disappointments, and longing that characterize your deficit. But, you will be unable to benefit from any interventions until you are free. Freedom is not just to count yourself as deserving of something better or different as Eve did in the story. Freedom is to recognize the power of working with others to actualize you. Stop worrying about whether you belong and whether others will accept you. Stop worrying about what others want. What you have is yours to offer. The potential benefit of that sharing is in the relationship—what you have added to what I bring.

Your potential productivity is beyond the consideration of your deficit. If you had to do this alone, it would make sense to be preoccupied with your deficit. But, a focus on collaboration means that you do not have to have all the answers, all the gifts, and have it all together.

Self-actualization enables you to reason and feel more abstract conceptions such as morality and creativity. Self-transcendence enables you to construct a more collective vision and realize that your individual potential expands exponentially with each like-minded person who joins toward your common cause.

At each level of Maslow's hierarchy, you are charged with actualizing the motivation to be your best self. The higher the level, the more your expression of actualization requires the ability to focus on relationships. Higher levels require you to see beyond yourself and your perceived deficits to celebrate your contribution, and combine it with my contribution.

Maslow (1943) conducted a biographical analysis of people he felt were self-actualizers. He uncovered a number of traits that fit these individuals. As you look through the list of traits, you quickly realize that adherence to these traits would mean a constant state of self-development. At first glance, you may see this constant development as chaotic. But, remember that the deficit needs have all been secured. The development "chaos" is opportunity to identify the fake, solve problems and inconsistencies, support responsible actions, enjoy solitude, rely on self, resist enculturation, value diversity, genuinely engage others, deepen relationships, laugh at yourself, accept yourself, be yourself, wonder and explore, create, and see yourself as a piece of a larger puzzle.

Deficits may be keeping you from being your best right now. You may be stressed by financial pressures, fear of physical danger, relationship pain, low confidence, or low respect. Other chapters in this text deal with those deficits. Let us deal with the deception that keeps you in deficit thinking even when you are, by all objective assessments, ready for self-actualization.

The deception of redirection is your focus on role stability as the foundation of success rather than role development. You interpret the natural uncertainty and consistent newness of self-actualization as an indication that you have not arrived at a point of stability. Let us work through your mis-education and fears toward a new understanding of risk as the foundation of your continued success. Not gambling but investment.

Investment: Paths to Certainty

If you knew that paying five dollars now would ensure twenty dollars next week, you would most likely excitedly hand over the five dollars. If your first response is that you do not have the five dollars, you are still in a deficit thinking mode. Your currency is not just money. If you knew that an investment of two hours per week would result in residual income for you and your family, you would most likely be motivated to find that time in your week.

Each choice you are faced with involves investment and return. A farmer would say sowing and reaping. Whatever seeds you plant, you can expect to grow into plants. If you plant fear, suspicions, and worry, expect to grow fearfulness, mistrust, and anxiety. If you plant thoughtfulness, actions, and risk, expect to grow structure, results, and reward. The effects of sowing and reaping in your life are both physical and psychological. Relationships are affected by what you sow, and the reaping determines your reality.

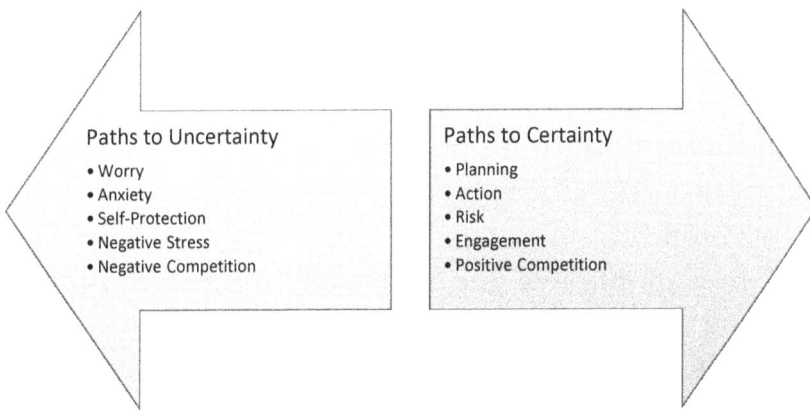

Paths to Uncertainty
- Worry
- Anxiety
- Self-Protection
- Negative Stress
- Negative Competition

Paths to Certainty
- Planning
- Action
- Risk
- Engagement
- Positive Competition

Paths to Uncertainty include Worry, Anxiety, Self-Protection, Negative Stress, and Negative Competition.

Paths to Certainty involve Planning, Action, Risk, Engagement, and Positive Competition.

Invest Planning not Worry

Contrary to the belief of some, worry is not a necessary condition of maturity. You can retain the expectant nature of youth— the utopia of perfection without the problems. Maturity means that you now have the power to create the conditions for that utopian ideal to become reality. This is not the fallacy of thinking you live in a perfect world. It is the knowledge that your actions have an impact on the world.

Rather than *worrying* about the seemingly inevitable challenges that you may come up against, *plan* for them. Take ownership. Take control. A well-thought out plan will embrace all the "worries" that can be conceived. The plan will also allow for unforeseen problems by including a measure of flexibility.

Relationships that feed you and those that offer real potential problems are both important in developing a good plan. Listen to those that you love and respect, but also reflect on the insight of the voices of those who do not agree with you. Fearfulness and mistrust keep potentially beneficial relationships from blossoming. Consider the value of inner circles of influence, extra circles of access, and other circles of insight.

Circles of influence guide you with support and challenge. They extend your internal dialogue and question you. These inner circles have access to hurt you at times, but the pruning results in your growth. Count on these relationships to be consistent reflections on your plan.

Circles of access are those relationships that represent connections to markets and other circles. These relationships are not as close, but their purpose is clear. Do not consider them as "family" though they may use those terms. Circles of access exist for your utilization. Factor the ebb and flow cycle of these relationships into your plan.

Circles of insight may offer no relationship at all. Their value is in the perspective they offer. Too often, you have dismissed alternate perspectives as haters, detractors, contrarians, and bitter rivals. It is time that you realize the value of the self-reflection these perspectives motivate. The ability to question yourself is vital to creating the insight that fuels inspiration. Your circles of insight may only be out to distract you, but you have the power to turn their venom into medicine.

Still other insight exists that you can learn from. These are neither friend nor foe. They simply offer experience and an example for you to watch. Notice the mistakes and disappointments that caused them to think that your plan will fail. A good plan includes attention to the usefulness of failure in the short term. Unforeseen things happen, but live within the reality that consistent, smart work pays off. You could be wrong. The virtue in being wrong is in the learning, to be able to use failure in the short term to ensure sustainable success in the long term.

Invest Action not Anxiety

Anxiety is an unsustainable response to stress. Anxiety can exacerbate a number of physical ailments—even prolonging the natural healing process. I talked with a 21 year old who expressed some anxiety about the speed at which she was expected to grow up. She spoke of her perception that others were more adult than her. She saw professionals that knew more than her.

She and you have something in common. You grieve the loss of youth—that feeling that you are not ultimately responsible. Someone else pays the bills. Someone else completes the applications. That time is no more. It is you who is responsible now. You are also frustrated that others seem to have what you do not yet have: a confidence, intentionality, and purpose. You hesitate unsure whether you can compete. At this point, your fear is in the place where competence should reside. Your hesitance is simply a lack of knowledge. Action requires that you get the knowledge you need in order to do what you are gifted to do. Feed your gift. You can learn from those around you that appear to be more advanced.

In response to anxiety, action has two important additional considerations. First, do you. Do not seek to replicate me or other professionals, even idols and role models. Watching and learning is useful, but take the time to discover your uniqueness. See my HOW without being preoccupied with my WHAT.

Second, the act of overcoming fear looks like courage, capability, and intelligence to everyone watching. It is not true that I am more advanced. I simply have more practice standing against my fears. Practice standing against yours, and you will display the same apparent brilliance that I display.

It is true that you cannot be him. You cannot look like her. His talents are not yours. Her gift is not yours. At this moment, she may be more accomplished than you. A focus on denying these current realities will only result in frustration. Faking it will not lead to making it. Be you...the best you that you know. And, seek to learn more about you and your expertise. You do not have to know everything. You are only responsible for your expertise.

Sustainable action is to cultivate positive self-talk that supports your activity rather than internal dialogue that feeds your anxiety. Often, you are your most vocal source of anxiety. You have so much to do. That is what you tell yourself. I challenge you to test everything—even your messages to yourself. Rather than continually stating that you are busy, become busy. Become active.

Set the number for the things you must accomplish. Make a list of the things you have to do. The list is often not as long as your level of anxiety would suggest. Prioritize. The tasks are often not as dire as you first insist. Schedule. Some items are not due until next week or next month. Set time deadlines for yourself. Be quick not perfect. Draft out long projects in advance of the due date. Small contributions over time will result in task completion. Build a first draft, and revise afterward. Stop. Reflect after 24 hours. Then, edit and finish. In the face of action, fear gives way to confidence.

It is important that you begin to see time as an opportunity to build something substantial. Time, like other supposed enemies, has utility. Order your action. Do the hard things first. Do the simples things next. And, whether you take that advice or not, do something until you get it done. It is not cheating to do the things that you like, and get them done even when it is not the order of your list.

Invest Risk not Self-Protection

Risk is not the opposite of self-protection. Risk is more precisely defined economically and socially as the expectation of reward. Work is required if you are to expect a reward. When I say to you, "Higher risk. Higher reward," I am challenging you to work with purpose and expectation, not just blindly trusting in something you know nothing about. But, risk is related to self-protection, because your resistance to my challenge is based in your inability to see a reward resulting from your work. You believe it is better to be safe and unfulfilled rather than to risk. Let me be the first to enlighten you: Your inability to see a reward resulting from your work is an indication that you need more information. Investigate work that produces rewards. You set the limit and the definition of your success.

Risk begins with you. I am not asking you to push beyond what you can handle. I am asking you to push beyond what is comfortable and safe for you. Not to trust blindly, but to research the opportunities and create a plan of action. The right risk will be natural to you. It is your gift. Feed it with more information. Learn about it.

Know the odds. Inform yourself about the markets that you may explore. If you are selling goods, you need ready buyers. If you are providing a service, you have to be filling a felt need. You must know what your competition is doing. You must also know what value you add. You may also consider what complementary products or services you may offer.

Mind the company you keep. Know what messages you are receiving from your peers, potential customers, family, and other stakeholders. Judge the value of the influences by whether or not they challenge you to be better. It does not matter how they present challenges, it only matters that you are better because of the challenge. Know that often, others exaggerate the difficulty of a task in order to build their own ego. Easy task does not necessarily mean that the task is not a risk.

Know the goals you have in mind. Define success for you. Rarely is success as simple as "being comfortable," but just as rare is success as grandiose as selling 100,000 units. You often ask yourself, "What do I need to be comfortable?" Comfort most likely has more to do with relationship than the risk we are discussing. Modest material goals typically include a house, a car, loans paid, money in the bank. Success for you then, is the figure it takes to secure those materials. Risk is expecting those materials to result from your work. Investment is to leverage those materials—that comfort—to build sustainable success.

Invest Engagement not Stress

Let me clear up a misconception for you. Stress is not a noun. It is a verb. People, situations, deadlines, challenges are all stressors, but stress is what you do when faced with a stressor. Stress is your reaction. Through your actions in response to stressors you have often said, "I'm going to stress." But, what will you do next time? "I'll stress then too." But, we need to do something. "Well, I'm stressing!" you continue to say.

When you are faced with obstacles, uncertainty, or pressures, your body naturally responds. If the stressor is intense enough, adrenaline starts to flow. This hormone may give you the sensation of nervousness offering the classic fight or flight option. When yours and my success are on the line, I say engage. Rather than run from the challenge, engage in the new experience. Collect yourself. Learn about the challenge. Connect with your support system. Set your goals. This outline is the process of engagement.

The biological reaction you display in response to stressors gives you the ability to do things both physically and mentally that may have been difficult without it. Your endurance is heightened. Your mental acuity increases. You may have only experienced this in response to tight deadlines. You have come to believe that it is the pressure that makes you great. You say, "I do my best work under pressure." Foolishness! If you can do good work at the last minute, imagine the great work you can do with more time. The outline for great work is simple: Collect yourself, Learn, Connect, and Set Goals.

Collect Yourself. The key is discipline—to engage that biological reaction on demand. You must see the outline for greatness and turn stressors into waypoints. This is collecting yourself. Bring your biological functions into submission to your will.

Learn. Gather the information you need in order to understand the work. Talk to others about their experience with similar challenges. Review what approaches make sense to you. Move from simply working harder to working smarter.

Connect. The single most predictive characteristic of success is support. Build a system of support that fits for the work at hand. Always rely on your mentor. Also, engage content experts and consultants.

Set Goals. Now that you know what you are working with, list goals that are unique to you. Being realistic is important, but not as important as reflecting you in the work. Challenge yourself and recognize the power of building incrementally toward larger goals. Plan in the context of the time you have and the eventual benefit expected.

Invest Positive Competition not Negative Competition

From an early age, you have always wanted to win. Your life experiences have changed your expectations and your habits toward winning. But, your default response to competition has stayed the same. You often speak about "proving her wrong." You are happy to rebut, "He does not know me. I am capable of much more."

I am asking you to change your definition of winning. Winning is bringing out the best in others. The best way to do that is to be your best, every moment, every task. You must also change your approach to competition. You are not competing in order to have what I have or to be like her. You are competing in order to bring out the best in you, me, and her. Competition, used wisely, is a complement to internal motivation. The result is your second wind—the ability to achieve beyond what you could do alone.

Definitions of winning and competition are not the most important change I want you to make. Most importantly, I want you to recapture the expectation that you will win. Disappointments and obstacles have contributed to a personality of individualism, habits of isolation, and motivation steeped in negative competition. You have a choice. Consider that collective activities do exist, interactions can be supportive, and competition can be positive.

Collective activities are tasks that you can share with others. You have been told that true expertise knows without any prompting.

This is only partly true. Expertise knows, but the development of expertise is often a function of like-minded people collectively sharing ideas and tasks. It is in the brainstorming and the doing that new methods take shape.

Vygotsky suggested that we become ourselves through others. This is true in your traditional supportive interactions, but also in your antagonistic relationships. The key observation is your reaction to the other. Others can motivate you to prove them, but the interaction may also provide an important reminder to pause and consider your actions, thoughts, and meaning making.

Positive competition is born out of the reality experienced when you are at your best. Collaboration is not just working together on a specific shared goal. It is sharing a goal. The enemy you and your foes have in common is failure. See that the competition that you may have resented is nothing more than an expression of respect. The others who you have assessed to be preoccupied with you are really targeting their own fears. No competitor worries about the opposition that has no momentum. As you move from potential to momentum, you will realize greater competition. Continue with purpose and the knowledge that each stride you take encourages the other. Each advance of the other signals motivation to you. Undergirding the competition is the certainty of reward. No other can wrest your trophy. Because of your disappointments and obstacles, you have fashioned an expertise that is uniquely yours. The product you will distribute, if it is truly your product, cannot be duplicated by any other.

CHAPTER 3
COUNTERFEITING

Sacred concepts misinterpreted and misapplied.
And the serpent said unto the woman, You shall not surely
die... Genesis 3:4

Deceptions Case Study: 2 of 3

The ancient text continues the story of Eve and the Serpent. Eve has been redirected from seeing her existence as freedom toward perceiving her choices to be limited. Eve now stands explaining what the creator had instructed her and Adam, "If we do not follow these instructions, we will die." The serpent says to Eve in effect, "You will not die. You will be free." The serpent did not lie to her. He told her a truth that matched with her current understanding of the question at hand. Eve was already in an erroneous thought pattern, seeking a freedom she already possessed. Her current thought pattern meant that she would discount the genuine article of freedom even as she was presented with it. Eve could no longer distinguish between freedom and bondage. The instructions given by the creator ensured a life of freedom. Eve was searching for confirmation, a search that heralded its death.

You, like Eve, naturally want to be self-actualized. But, again like Eve, you seek appearances and confirmation rather than understanding and expression. Abraham Maslow communicated it plainly in his 1993 edition of *The Farther Reaches of Human Nature*. The self-actualized individual exhibits concentration, growth choice, self-awareness, honesty, judgment, self-development, peak experiences, and lack of ego defenses. Even if you have learned to exhibit the above toward role development and investment, a central question remains. Do you know that genuine freedom is experience, not a mere pronouncement?

Experience requires risk. You cannot test a certain condition without risking a move from your current state of being. It is risk that separates the counterfeit characteristic from the real characteristic. When the goal is to maintain your safety more than it is to participate genuinely in community, counterfeits result. As an ego defense, counterfeiting is to count the appearance (or pronouncements) as evidence of success as opposed to requiring the work, competence, partnership, and risk as evidence of success.

Characteristics of Self-Actualizers

Your miseducation through faulty, imperfect examples means that you may misinterpret and misapply certain concepts highlighted as characteristics of self-actualizers. Because you see the end results of hard work and growth choices, you mistake the appearance of success for real success. This mistake is perpetuated through imperfect examples so much so that you now define success by appearance rather than the substance of experience. These counterfeits extend to all the characteristics of self-actualizers. The result is your ignorance to the fact that success requires character. You set your goals on having rather than experiencing. You want to plant and reap instantaneously without the periods of watering, sun, and growth.

In an attempt to re-educate you, I have translated Maslow's original list (1970, pp. 153-172) to reflect more up-to-date language as follows: Reality-centered, Problem-centered, Process-centered, Private, Autonomous, Unique, Culturally Competent, Compassionate, Intimate, Amicable, Tolerant, Authentic, Inspired, Creative, and Successful. Let us discuss the counterfeits that may perpetuate your deception.

The deception detailed in this section is termed "counterfeiting." Counterfeits are not opposites of the character traits of self-actualizers. They are words that have become synonymous with the character traits, but whose practice outside of the values of individual responsibility and promotion of community yield unsustainable results.

Reality-centered Counterfeit: Realistic

Reality-centered is unchanged from Maslow's phrasing. According to Maslow, as a reality-centered individual, you have the ability to differentiate fake from genuine. I add that you also possess the ability to identify your own giftedness and the gifts of others. You also have a keen sense of the emotional depth of others—an awareness of those who are not genuine.

The counterfeit of the reality-centered individual is the realistic individual. If you are realistic, you experience giftedness as negative competition and seek to disguise your own ambition by pointing out the ambition of others. You thereby improperly focus the attention on a false humility that serves to stifle the individual contributions of others in the group.

Insecure, you seek to deny that individual gifts are important to group success preferring rather to proffer the false duality of individuality versus collectivism. You believe that individual giftedness can only lead to conceit. You mask your own insecurity, conceit, and lack of perceived ability by expertly degrading the ideas and contributions of others. You rarely have an original idea, but you are quick to counterpoint the original ideas of another. When called on your insecurity and lack of contribution you retort, "I'm just being realistic," or "I'm just playing devil's advocate." In polite company, you may be applauded for being realistic. The truth is you are a hater disguising your own reckless ambition.

To experience the genuine reality-centered characteristic, be the best you can be, and allow me to be my best. Our best ideas on the same team will yield greater outcomes than my best ideas or your best ideas alone. My gift does not diminish the brilliance of your gift. If my skill set is best for the problem at hand, and I step forward, you must not stand in our way.

Problem-centered Counterfeit: Problem-focused

Problem-centered is unchanged from Maslow's phrasing. He suggests that the problem-centered individuals believe that life demands solutions. I add that, as a problem-centered individual, you explore inconsistencies in your life, and seek new knowledge with which to understand those inconsistencies.

The counterfeit is problem-focused. If you are problem-focused, you have a keen awareness of failures and shortfalls without the necessary motivation to seek solutions. You do not bother to seek new knowledge. You operate as if the recognition of the shortfall is the solution—a victory within itself. The person who predicts failure is not a productive team position. We know that failure looms. How do we, as a group, make failure less likely and success more likely?

Problem-focused, you seek to advance the false duality of perfection or imperfection. But, perfection can neither be achieved in isolation nor achieved once and for all. Perfection is a collective process. In human systems, it is incremental and multi-faceted. That means, our perfection will be the outcome of multiple solutions maintained over time. This also means that failure in one solution does not mean ultimate failure. We learn. We apply that learning to the next proposed solution. "Perfection is a myth," you might say. It is only a myth to those who fail to realize that anything worth having must be maintained.

Problem-centered, you address each problem as it reveals itself. You are proactive in your approach to challenges that wait on the horizon. Perfection is not a destination or an end result. You recognize that perfection is a commitment to solutions and collective activity each of us combining our strengths to address the next challenge.

Process-centered Counterfeit: Process-focused

Process-centered is an attempt to clarify what Maslow termed a "different perception of means and ends." With this, Maslow sought to convey contentment and valuing of the journey, in addition to the outcomes. I add that, as a process-centered individual, you maintain consistent values in regard to process and outcomes. You make choices by a consistent standard: to violate my principles on the way to achieving my goals, even altruistic goals, is unacceptable.

The counterfeit of the process-centered individual is the process-focused individual. You give attention to the process, but have limited vision and expectation that any end results from your actions. You are always doing, but never producing. As a result, the

42

group is hindered from building on successes and learning from failures. Since you unwittingly continue in a process without outcomes, you are unable to share the how with others.

A myopic and incomplete vision causes you to continually think that success just happens, without any necessary attention beyond what you are doing right now. You are content that a bird in the hand is worth two in the bush. You mask your myopia in fatalism or feigned pragmatism. "If it's God's will," or "I'm just enjoying what I'm doing right now," you say. But, you have left much that was within your power undone. To others, you look like you are the picture of serenity. But, you have neglected to identify outcomes and thus the building blocks to your continual success. You remain blissfully ignorant as to whether tomorrow's choices contradict the actions of today. Once you happen upon success, you will quiet your conscience then, conveniently forgetting the contradictions you wrought and the problems you created for me and others along your way.

To be truly process-centered, set a vision for yourself that is beyond what you can currently achieve. Plan systematically to accomplish that vision, making your expectations known. Enjoy the journey. Use both small successes and failures to clarify your expectations. Continue to develop, but also challenge yourself to learn more and take risks. The farmer who sows into the ground expects a harvest in due season. She toils not for the planting, but for the harvest. With each success, reap the consistency you have sown.

Private Counterfeit: Isolated

Private is a comfort with and purposefulness in being alone. Maslow termed it "need for privacy." To Maslow's expression of meaning, I add the construct of self-development. Individuals enjoy a break from the expectations of other people, but the central question is in the extent to which your interactions were expressions of yourself or reflections of the expectations of others. It is important to separate yourself from community with the intent to return to community with a fresh perspective and a surer sense of self.

The counterfeit of private is isolated. As an isolated individual, you refuse to participate in social discourse that proposes to shape you and others. You may prefer to shape others only, so that you are perceived as righteous or wise. You may seek to place yourself above others clinging to a sense of safety. As a result, others in the group become guarded, and the opportunity for authenticity and development is lost.

You want people to believe that you are a thinker, deep in thought. But, your communications never place your perceptions on the line. You are never caught in self-introspection or doubt. You are certain of every utterance, sure of every idea, and clear about the failure of others when your ideas do not pan out. You resist and outright refuse to share your motivations and your intentions with the group. "You can't tell everyone your ideas," or "Never let them see you sweat," you are often heard to say. Acquaintances may be tolerant while they work to figure you out. But, once it is clear that you never risk, they will not risk with you. Your intention is to show yourself as a leader, but also as infallible.

To be truly private requires that time alone is time spent gaining self-awareness. Success follows when you develop both individually and within the group. You ask yourself the challenging questions. You do not just assume that the knee-jerk reactions you have to situations are your true response. Time away from the pressures of human interaction is opportunity to consider scenarios and different courses of action. You consider the alternate outcomes resulting from your choice to react in a different way. You explore the options. In your decided approach, you seek consistency between the person you want to be and the person your actions reveal. You return to community ready to engage.

Autonomous Counterfeit: Skeptical

Autonomous means relying on your own experiences and judgments to provide context for new information. Maslow described this quality as "independent of culture and environment." To Maslow's meaning, I add two concepts: reciprocity and engagement. Reciprocity joined to autonomy recognizes the give and take between the individual and the cultural environment. Engagement joined to autonomy requires you to actively seek that give and take. You cannot sustainably define yourself by the community, but it is important to realize how your environment shapes you as well as your opportunity to shape your environment.

The counterfeit of autonomy is skepticism. As a skeptical individual, you pick and choose among new information counteracting calls to personal responsibility and the duty to contribute to the common good. You often speak of "gut feelings" and anecdotal evidence that contradicts information garnered from multiple sources. Often, this character is so practiced that you are surprised when asked to produce objective evidence. You are ever-ready to diminish, contradict, or belittle the opinion and learning of the other. You often insist on your opinion as if it is fact. Rather than citing reliable sources, you always have some "inside information" from people you know. "I've heard that this is the case," you are often heard to say.

You strive to be the voice of caution—to be received as wise and self-reliant. But, your contribution to the group is only an attempt to self-aggrandize—to make yourself an authority. At first, the group may act on your slight evidence due to your insistence, but your lie will gradually be ferreted by the presentation of evidence to the contrary. What is more, your relationships with others will fail due to your refusal to take responsibility and your flippant attitude toward the group setback that your skepticism has caused.

To be truly autonomous, use your own experiences as a funnel, not a filter. Review all new information without prejudice or predilection. Recognize that your growth and learning occurs in the context of information gleaned from the culture and environment. Your decisions about action result from an objective assessment of the best route for you as individually responsible for your choices. Also insist that your success contribute to the success of the group. Realize that others are capable of similar growth and learning by information. Your question is not whether another has grown, but whether she has been informed.

Unique Counterfeit: Contradictory

Unique is a reasoned individual contribution in the context of the larger culture. Maslow states that these individuals resisted enculturation. In clarifying Maslow's meaning, I focus more on the action of the individual contribution rather than the resistance. Think first of your responsibility to yourself, then reason your contribution to society. Our collective needs and donations provide the pull and push that powers culture.

The counterfeit of uniqueness is contradictory. As a contradictory individual, you state contradictions to the brainstorms of others as the devil's advocate. You quote common contradictions to accepted culture. You are active in your intention to present yourself as free from the influences of culture, yet your contribution is often cliché or otherwise trite. You want the group to focus on you and your supposed uniqueness, but your contradictions only serve to cause spectacle and frustrate group innovation.

You want to contribute to the group discussion, but you do not evidence the reasoning and foundation of information that would support your pretend wisdom. You possess the boldness and the agency that are characteristic of uniqueness, but you lack the thoughtfulness and the defensible knowledge base. You erroneously think that innovation means denying that the decisions of the past have worth. Because of this missed learning opportunity, you often suggest repeating past failures under new names.

To be truly unique is to actively contribute to the creation of culture with a reasoned approach to supporting or redirecting individual and collective actions. Uniqueness is based in knowledge of self, the contribution of others, the mechanism of culture, and the impact of culture on behavior. Unique individuals are able to experiment with new inputs to the mechanism. They model the resultant behaviors in ways that articulate interrelatedness and options for the group.

Culturally Competent Counterfeit: Disengaged

Cultural Competence is rooted in appreciation of difference. Maslow described this character as "democratic values." He sought to describe individuals who possessed openness to ethnic and individual variety. I reinterpret Maslow's observations, and rename this character cultural competence. Cultural competence maintains the openness to difference and adds an intentional support of complementary relationships. In addition to valuing the contributions of others, cultural competence presupposes an awareness of the deficits and abilities within yourself and the deficits and abilities within those you would collaborate with. This awareness is the basis for productive collaboration.

The counterfeit of cultural competence is the disengaged character. As a disengaged individual, you lack a connection between your deficits and abilities and the deficits and abilities of the other. You are not interested enough in the other to explore mutual benefit that can result in increased capacity for the other or even for you. Often, your calculation is a one-sided recognition of what the other can provide to you. You expect that the other should be happy to be included in your plans. Without an open discussion of needs and contributions clearly shared among the group, you diminish the practical incentives toward collaboration. When participants voice deficit needs, you rethink the wisdom of the collaboration and may seek separation.

People initially see you as a ready collaborator and a gracious host. But, your true character is displayed when your goals are threatened by the deficits of the others. You begin to question the collaboration and the commitment of the others. You state, "I tried to include them, but it didn't work out." You have nothing but "good" things to say about failed collaborators, but the compliments are back-handed and evidence your disengagement more than the failures of the other.

To be truly culturally competent is to realize that partnership is a sharing of destiny and history. The vigor and interest typically experienced in the initial convening activity should include assessment of deficits and historical development in addition to the goals of the current collaboration.

Realize that the other may not be aware of the deficits and solutions. Your commitment in collaboration is to contribute to solutions by informing yourself of the needs of the other and maintaining reflectiveness about how you advanced to the position you currently inhabit. An opportunity exists for you and me to help each other achieve. We can help each other identify deficits and solutions that we would not have identified in isolation and could not have solved alone.

Compassionate Counterfeit: Histrionic

Maslow used the term Gemeinschaftsgefühl to describe a character encompassing social interest, compassion, and humanity. I interpret the term and recast the character as compassionate. This term focuses on the commitment to work collaboratively to achieve shared outcomes.

The counterfeit of compassionate is histrionic. As a histrionic character, you have a superficial concern for others that wanes with time. You are initially perceived as caring, but you soon appear melodramatic. Histrionic characters are typically overwrought during greetings, celebrations, expressions of sadness, or other opportunities for emotional display. The intention is to meant demonstrate interest physically, not just communicate it verbally.

Interpersonal interactions of the histrionic character, over time, are revealed as performances. You often give away your drama soon after interactions. You often reveal to supposed friends who are left to wonder if your interactions with them are as lacking as your interactions with others. In the group, you push an agenda that seems centered in concern for a population. But, your concern is not consistent in addressing all the areas of need required for self-sufficiency or sustainable success of the population. You refuse to commit yourself personally to ensuring the wellbeing of the population (or the group for that matter). This reveals that you only seek to use the "concern" to forward your own agenda at the expense of the population and the group.

To be truly compassionate, you represent a character of collaboration toward the greater good. Your commitment is demonstrated in your engagement in the discussion of shared outcomes as well as some measure of personal sacrifice. You commit to being an active agent in solutions. You maintain this commitment by continuing the conversation, nurturing the collaboration.

Intimate Counterfeit: Indulgent

Maslow discussed "intimate personal relations" as a character that values closeness to fewer friends rather than shallow relationships with many. I focus on the intimacy term in Maslow's phrase to isolate and expand on the deep trust relationship that it describes.

The counterfeit of intimate is indulgent. As an indulgent character, you offer too much of yourself. You are unaware of the full set of options that communicate and sustain intimacy. Often, you have problems with sexualizing individual relationships with interactions that misrepresent trust. In groups, you tend toward discussions that are too personal, revealing information that most feel should be kept private.

You want people to perceive you as engaged and engaging, but you perceive a false duality. You think that the only options are to be an open book with no secrets or to be a stuffy social derelict. Trust is thwarted because the core of your interaction is to fulfill your own emptiness. It is more precise to term your behavior as chatty. You often lack appropriate boundaries to the point of over sharing.

To be truly intimate is to engage seeking a deeper knowledge of the choice behavior of others—a genuine interest in why people do the things they do. Intimacy involves less talking and more listening. Truly intimate relationships take many forms based in conversations in which an understanding of the other is increased. Intimacy is not just sex. In fact, true intimacy does not have to be related to sexuality or discussed in sexual terms.

Amicable Counterfeit: Patronizing

Amicable describes a character with a sense of humor that engages others. Maslow termed this sense of humor as "unhostile." He sought to describe a character that prefers to joke at his expense rather than embarrassing others. I only simplify Maslow's phrase to one word: amicable.

The counterfeit of amicable is patronizing. As a patronizing individual, you get the mechanics of self-effacing, but you always seek to be the center of attention—as if to be lauded for your humility. Your attempts at humor begin with jokes about yourself, but end with backhanded compliments directed at others. In groups, you promote your status as the alpha leader with condescension that diminishes the contributions of others while appearing to encourage them. You are fond of saying things like, "That's not your strong suit. You should do this instead."

It is often obvious that you are trying to be funny. Your attempts are flawed because your humor is not participatory. Your intention is to appear down-to-earth and approachable, but interactions often end with the revelation of your character as insecure and condescending.

To be truly amicable is to be able to laugh at yourself, to find humor in the human condition. Your humor invites others to participate and take themselves less seriously. You have the ability to support humor in humorous instances rather than forcing humor into serious conversations. Individuals leave your presence with a strong sense of the humor in life rather than a sense of you as the comedian.

Tolerant Counterfeit: Superficial

Tolerant is a character marked by acceptance of self and others just as Maslow communicated. To this, I add that this character allows you to change your definition of self and grow over time. This character is also marked by the ability to risk. Being wrong or unpopular is an acceptable risk if it brings others into the interaction.

The counterfeit of tolerant is superficial. As a superficial character, you lack the engagement that enables true analysis of yourself and objective evaluation of others. You miss opportunities to challenge yourself to be better. You allow others to be mediocre rather than point out failures because blindness to their failure enables blindness to your own ineptitude.

You approach your choices as all or nothing. You think that the only choices are to be totally accepting or to be intolerant. You are often heard saying, "To each his own," or "As long as it doesn't affect me." You miss opportunities to grow yourself and participate in the growth of others because you never risk being wrong. You never risk landing on the unpopular side of what is "polite" or "considerate."

To be truly tolerant, you engage. Your interaction is less about determining right and wrong, and more about supporting the idea that growth and change is possible. Discussions of growth and change, when first applied to you, can yield new insights into how we all might work together toward success. Just because you believed yourself to be something last year, does not mean that new information cannot inform a new belief this year. You apply this allowance to yourself, and risk that others will not agree.

Authentic Counterfeit: Arrogant

Authentic is characterized by a well-defined identity and role in environment. Maslow termed this spontaneity and simplicity. He explained that this character preferred being themselves rather than being pretentious. I clarify this language to place it squarely in the context of research on identity formation and social role definition.

The counterfeit of authentic is arrogant. As an arrogant individual, you lack a sense of self in the context of others. You seek to define yourself as separate from others. In this way, you do not have to evaluate the ethics or congruence of walking the talk. You self-protect in the group by thinking yourself smarter than the others. Rather than seeing this as an opportunity to share your knowledge, you decide that only you can understand.

You want people to see you as self-confident. But, we soon realize that you have little awareness of others. Your contribution is not to the group. It is simply an attempt to reject your feelings of loneliness. You often say, "I could explain it, but they will not understand." Rather than recognizing your deficit in communication, you adopt the view that you are superior and therefore exempt from any collective social definition of self.

To be truly authentic, you embrace both your strengths and your weaknesses. You realize that who you are is only partially defined by what you know and who you know. Your social role is also important. Social role is what you contribute to the group. Authenticity is commitment to the requirements of your contribution and consistent participation in the discourse.

Inspired Counterfeit: Punctilious

Inspired is a character that explores origins, present realities, and potential futures. Maslow used the phrase "freshness of appreciation" to describe this character. He explained that this character possessed the ability to see things (even small things) with a sense of wonder. I add that this sense of wonder motivates action and offsets fear.

The counterfeit of inspired is punctilious. As a punctilious character, you attend to the form requirements of behavior without an intrinsic connection to people. Your individual relationships are often awkward to onlookers with inappropriate intimacy for the relationship at hand. In the group, you often trade in humor and feigned concern in an attempt to show yourself to be caring as opposed to cold and singularly focused on the set agenda.

You want people to see you as interested in them and engaged. On closer inspection, you are just going through the motions of polite interaction. Your interest does not extend beyond the formalities of human contact. Your focus is the agenda you adopted in order to maintain your safety in the presence of multiple points of view. You cannot take the time to consider the value of the other's contribution. Exploring beyond your agenda is to risk too much.

To be truly inspired is to recognize the value of diverse contributions and the opportunity represented by collaboration. Inspiration is not only the reality that you are not alone. It is the realization that the process of human interaction yields exponential returns. The commonalities and differences found between us lessen the load and create opportunities that were impossible for you to conceive of by yourself. The more people we invite to the table, the more possibilities avail themselves…if you engage.

Creative Counterfeit: Indecisive

Creative is a character that brings together form and art to create. Maslow also used the term creative. Creative characters, according to Maslow, were inventive and original. I add an emphasis on the process of creativity to the definition. Creative characters combine a search for knowledge with a respect for the empowerment of self-reflection.

The counterfeit of creative is indecisive. As an indecisive individual, you rely on external pressures or uncertainty to determine projects or goals. It is indecisive because you do not take responsibility for the process. You rationalize that if you wait until the last minute, you always have an excuse for why the product is not perfect. This also makes it impossible for you to work with others.

You want others to see you as original, but you take your cues from the pressure rather than from a careful meditation on form and art. You are often heard to say, "I put that together at the last minute" or "I do my best work under pressure." This is only half true. You do perform at the last minute, but you fail to take the time to consider the quality of the work that could have been created over a longer period of time.

To be truly creative you will build each product as an exercise in knowledge gathering and self-reflection. Rather than last minute excuses, you will stand behind the work that you produce. You will challenge yourself to learn more about the craft and the methods of your expertise. You will reflect on what you have learned and place it in the context of who you are and the contribution that you would like to make to the world around you.

Successful Counterfeit: Revelous

Successful refers to a characteristic experience of achievement. Maslow described this character as "peak experiences." He talked about individuals who were able to seize opportunities to see themselves as small pieces of a larger puzzle. To Maslow's observations, I add the idea of small successes in the context of self-motivation.

Peak experiences are not always the completion of a goal. Small successes admonish you to look for the consistent and sustainable path. Success is not only in the destination, it is in the day-to-day approach toward goals.

The counterfeit of successful is revelous—a life characterized by revelry. As a revelous individual, you are characterized by highs and lows that threaten your consistency and sap your motivation. When you complete a task, you consider it an end, and celebrate disregarding the road still ahead. When you fail at a task, you fall into a funk, questioning the path you began.

People often see you as a rollercoaster of emotion. Because you put neither achievements nor failures in the context of a larger puzzle, you resort to the extreme reactions of what you think others expect. Your individual relationships are superficial because you are incapable of sharing your fit with others. The group subjugates you to either being the cheerleader or the voice of realism. Neither role is crucial to the team.

To be truly successful, you will see your gifts in the context of the abilities of others and the opportunities of the environment. As a successful individual, you realize that small successes build toward larger successes. This awareness keeps you internally encouraged and building. An awareness of the road ahead tempers your enthusiasm in order to stoke your endurance toward the completion of more challenging goals.

Counterfeits of Maslow's Translated Be Needs

Characteristic	Counterfeit (Individual/Group)
Reality-centered: Identify individual giftedness and emotional depth.	**Realistic (Insecure/ Hater)**: Denying the power of the individual contribution and desire to succeed.
Problem-centered: Explore inconsistencies to gain new knowledge.	**Problem-focused (Pessimistic/ Critical)**: Keen awareness of failures and shortfalls without awareness of solutions and lack of seeking new knowledge.
Process-centered: Consistent values in process and outcomes.	**Process-focused (Gullible/Unwitting): Pragmatic** Attention to process but blindness to the end expected or resulting from actions taken.
Private: Benefit self-development from solitude especially developing self-control.	**Isolated (Contemplative/Loner)**: Refusing to participate in the social interactions that result in development of self and others.
Autonomous: relying on your own experiences as a funnel not a filter; using self and community to process new information.	**Skeptical (Self-Reliant/Fearful)**: Picking and choosing new information counteracting personal responsibility and your contribution to the group.
Unique: contribute to culture with sound, consistent reasoning for supporting or redirecting individual and collective actions.	**Contradictory (Learned/Ignorant)**: Voicing often cliché or simple contradictions to accepted culture in order to appear learned or nonconformist.
Culturally Competent: Awareness of deficits and Valuing the contribution of others.	**Disengaged (Passive/Complacent)**: Lacking a connection between deficits, abilities present and outcomes that are possible.
Compassionate: Commitment to work in collaboration for shared outcomes.	**Histrionic (Concerned/Melodramatic)**: Having a superficial concern or waning interest.
Intimate: A deeper knowledge allowing for a deeper trust relationship.	**Indulgent (Engaged/Chatty):** Lacking appropriate boundaries **to the point of over sharing** .
Amicable: prefer to joke at your own expense.	**Patronizing (Self-Effacing/Fake)**: Interacting with an air of condescension.
Tolerant: Less focus on right and wrong, realizing that change is possible in yourself and others.	**Superficial (Considerate/Divested)**: An allowance of others due to a lack of risk in relationship.
Authentic: Well-defined identity and role in environment	**Arrogant (Self-confident/Self-absorbed)**: Lacking a sense of self in the context of others

Characteristic	Counterfeit (Individual/Group)
Inspired: Exploring origins, present, and potential futures.	**Punctilious (Interested/Formal):** Attending to the form requirements of behavior without intrinsic connection.
Creative: Bringing together form and art to create.	**Indecisive (Original/Indecisive):** Relying on external pressures or uncertainty to determine projects or goals.
Successful: Realizing that small successes build.	**Revelous (Bubbly/Superficial):** Lack of awareness of how the pieces fit together in the context of the larger community.

CHAPTER 4
RATIONALIZATION

Powers of reason misused.

Deceptions Case Study 3 of 3

The ancient text continues the story of Eve and the serpent. Eve's deception could not be completed without a lie. Yet, the lie was not told by the serpent in the story. The lie was formulated in the perception Eve had of her opportunity to become... to self-actualize. In the story, Eve, just after explaining what directions she was given, studied the tree. She evaluated the fruit. In her estimation, it was appetizing and attractive. When Eve began to rationalize, she was no doubt aware of the command given to her husband by the creator. "Do not eat from the tree of the knowledge of good and evil," was the command. The answer to the serpent's directive to eat was an emphatic, "No!" As the conversation and Eve's rationalization continued, the question was no longer, "Should I eat from this tree?" The question became a statement, "Becoming wise is a righteous pursuit." She further reasoned, "A god who would keep us from being self-actualized is himself wrong. That means that anything the creator commands cannot be trusted."

The lesson to be learned from this story is well below the surface of the supposed wrong choice. Right and wrong are too dualistic to provide important lessons. Consider determining whether your actions are sustainable or unsustainable.

In the story, reason is sustainable. Perception is sustainable. To question the lessons of the community that you grew up in is sustainable. The deception here is the rationalization that wisdom can be gained in an instant, absent from community. The need for immediate results, the desire to demonstrate independence, the disregard for process, all stem from an innate human reality. We each want to trust and to be sure that our trust is cherished.

Often, when faced with the option to trust others, your first instinct is to protect yourself. A decision to trust may result in pain, but it may also result in a success beyond what was possible for you alone. How can you distinguish between reason rooted in community and rationalization rooted in a protectionist trust only of yourself? This chapter answers this question with an informed approach to discernment—knowledge that is process-based, disciplined, discoverable, and organic.

Redefining

Process, Independence, Rightness, and Self

I do not know exactly what you were born into, but I do know for certain that what you are today, right now, is not comparable in achievement and acclaim to what you will be in the future. How can I be so certain? I am certain because a disciplined approach to any endeavor will yield results. A sustained contribution to your own success will free you from any deficiencies that present themselves as fears. Your deficiencies only outline the primary learning and relationships required for your success.

Your powers of intellect can be used against you. Pride can push you toward your own destruction. You must dispel the thought that you can achieve success on your own—that you are smarter or stronger than others only due to your uniqueness. Do not reason that, in yourself alone, you are wise. The value of your intellect and uniqueness is demonstrated in your contribution. Even if you are not celebrated in your current environment, that slight as motivation suggests that you can use the negative intentions of others to support your sustainable ends. Be they supportive or obstructive, realize that you do not achieve without others.

The most dangerous deception is the deception you perpetrate on yourself. Once you have begun to believe without hope of contradiction that your actions are honorable, you are most dangerous. Outside counsel is shrugged off. Voices from multiple sources and perspectives are disregarded. With fervor and passion, you do what you have purposed in your heart. Regardless of the lack of sustainability and consequences of your actions, you refuse to discern the deception.

More than a few methods exist in preparation for our self-deceit. As with other deceptions, they appear on the surface as desirable traits. Yet, without the principles of individual role definition combined with responsibility to community, seemingly desirable traits become seducers toward quick fixes and unsustainable gratification.

Notice the central deception in rationalization: your desire to achieve success equipped only with a short-term view of process, an irresponsible view of independence, a dualistic view of rightness, and a stifling outlook on self. Overcoming rationalization is overcoming the willful misinterpretation of process, independence, rightness, and yourself. It is a choice to realize success and self-actualization as a continuous process of becoming. It is a choice toward the goal of interrelated community.

Wanting To Have an Answer Now

Redefinition: the point of the *process* is perseverance not simple patience. Be ready!

You have been taught that the process requires patience. You wait until you are unable to sit any longer. You, then, make decisions of convenience in the context of your current knowledge motivated by your immediate desires. Your desire for a quick answer can seduce you into short cuts and suspect relationships. That same desire is a thirst for knowledge that keeps you searching, learning, and developing for a lifetime. Use that desire to motivate a determination toward preparedness.

Patience in the process, in truth, is an opportunity to work through the deficiencies you have. Practice a determined meditation—calm your anxiety through careful consideration of the inputs, the process, and potential consequences. Gain new knowledge through observation and reading. Maintain awareness. Seek out opportunities and surround yourself with productive individuals. Cultivate a state of preparedness. In time, your knowledge, role definition, and relationships result in your ability to create your own opportunities.

It is not imperative that you know the master plan. You only have to be clear on your role and your next step. You will not achieve success without the process. Enjoy the process rather than wasting time trying to circumvent it, or agonizing over the fact that the destination is unclear to you. Take pride in identifying your individual role and our collective responsibility. Be ready!

Wanting To Show Our Independence

Redefinition: the point of *independence* is
discipline not power. Let us move together!

You have been taught that independence is power. You seek to wield that power as an indication of your achievement. You, then, find yourself justifying your choices with apologies to those who counted on you. The motivation to set yourself apart can, unchecked, isolate you from community. Wanting to set yourself apart can also motivate you toward sustainable contributions to the community. Your uniqueness can steel you to the deceptions to which others fall prey. You can think beyond the current moment to see our common future.

Independence, in truth, is recognition of the power you have even in the absence of titles, positions, and hierarchy. It is the discipline to utilize power with purpose, always having a reasoned approach to action. It is determining the wise course by whether it achieves a collective vision and satisfies a consensus need.

You must learn to distinguish between those that can be trusted and those who cannot. It is true that you are powerful. The promise of community is that other lights combined with yours can illuminate a brighter future. This requires risk. But, this risk is not blind. Those who will combine with you in community will complement your contribution and demonstrate discipline just as you must.

As comfortable and safe as it is to believe the contrary, you are not alone in your quest to succeed. But, this does not diminish the fact that each choice is ultimately yours to make. The risks and investments are yours to live with. You hold responsibility for your choices, but your freedom to make those choices is in the context of a larger community. Purpose gives power. Discipline is power. When we move, let us move together.

Wanting To Know Finally

Redefinition: the point of *rightness* is discovery not proof. Let us explore the inconsistencies!

You have been taught that rightness is a settled question. You do not take time to discuss the questions at hand. In this way, you have no responsibility for inconsistencies. You are able to dismiss new information even before it is presented. You never have to explain when the calculation fails to add up to the expected value.

You seem very adept at designating those things that are forbidden to us. It seems that the commitment to be wise is a commitment NOT to participate in many things. This seclusion makes good sense to you because it seems that more "bad choices" exist than "good choices." You argue that to live by the allowances of freedom is to live reckless and without boundaries. You consider anyone who celebrates freedom as a lawless, wanton, and uncivilized individual.

The danger in your belief is not so much that you shy away from detrimental activity but that you decline from any risk at all. To suspend the finality of your judgments long enough to investigate a reality and explore new information is to admit that you do not know everything. Suspension of your belief in one ultimate truth is to admit that maybe your past lack of participation was a mistake. You may find disappointment realizing that you could have fed your inner child sustainably. You continue in your current understanding because you do not want that additional disappointment, and because you do not want to be wrong.

Rightness, in truth, is a social construction rooted in the norms of the group. The discussion of rightness is a discussion of sustainability and the long-term responsibility we all assume for the decisions we make today. When you observe inconsistencies, rightness is the motivation to explore the context, variables, procedures, and timing in order to reason through the unexpected results. Rightness reminds you that you have need of new information.

You must always remain open to integrating new information. Take responsibility for your decisions. Learn from them. But, do not define yourself by the information or the decisions. Being open to new information means being open to being wrong, accepting the consequences, and moving forward with the lessons learned. In this way, you are never condemned to be solely defined by your previous experiences or your prior choices. You are always learning. You have the opportunity in the next moment to choose differently. That next choice is what defines who you are.

This perspective is difficult because it requires that you allow others to choose and change. It may also extend and challenge you because it suggests a worldview that is less permanent. But, the reward is in the discovery and integration of lessons that add to your self-development. You will find that you engage more authentically. You explore with more wonder, and you genuinely appreciate diverse people and different ideas.

Wanting To Know Yourself for Yourself

Redefinition: the point of *role definition* is
discernment not infallibility. Grow organically!

You have been taught that you are singularly unique and required to strive toward perfection. You adopt an approach to the perfection question that either perpetuates a cycle of poor mental health, failed relationships, or both. You would rather be convinced rather than convicted. That way, you do not have to take responsibility for the choices you have made and the consequences that have resulted. You were just following the information you were given.

Your self-absorption is your excuse and your curse. According to you, you know yourself. But, your knowledge does not result in sustainable choices. Your knowledge results in over-thinking rather than doing. Your knowledge leaves you frozen and isolated.

Your excuse is solid. Because you know yourself, you do not place yourself in the position to explore new information. In effect, you refuse the need to grow in an area by steering away from situations that offer an opposing or more in-depth perspective. But, new and expanded information has a way of revealing itself regardless of your intentional ignorance. At that moment, you stand paralyzed, or worse, dissonant. You act out of a sense of obligation, shame, or political correctness rather than clear conviction. You rationalize that you were forced by the situation into a limited set of choices. Not so! You refused to prepare and contemplate your role toward a sustainable, responsible handling of new knowledge.

Perfection, in truth, is the role definition that can only be achieved in the context of others. The peak of human experience is discerning through the uncertainty of the multitude of "good" options. To know yourself is to challenge your internal conversations and your comfortable reactions, to question your answers and your certainties about yourself. To know yourself is to determine the knowledge, experiences, and relationships that motivate your growth. The challenge can certainly offer difficulty, but you gain from the stretching.

Life offers plateaus of arrival, but no end to the journey. You will make mistakes. You have made mistakes. You cannot redo much of what you have done, but you can purpose to engage in new experiences and formulate new directions and opinions. You can be sure of your choices based on the convictions you now hold. You can also, at the same time, be open and receptive to new information realizing that your current conviction could be unsustainable, incomplete, and only a piece of the larger puzzle. This realization is not a failure that signals despair, but a motivator toward continued exploration.

Faith. The Final Frontier.

Faith is the self-fulfilling prophecy spoken by your actions. It is your confidence in what you cannot see, combined with the preparation and sustained action toward what you hope to achieve. It is also a balance between fool-hardy wishful thinking and reality you can touch and take to the bank. Yet, faith is not the abstract, metaphysical wish, it has tangible elements. It just takes creativity, vision, and perseverance to connect the dots represented by those elements. Faith is as real as your will to live that reality.

Perhaps an example will help. You want to be a writer. You recognize that writing takes practice. You know that, each day, writers spend some time writing. You know that you need to improve your vocabulary. You know that you learn best by reading. Connect those dots to achieve your vision as a writer.

Set aside time each day to write. It could be in a journal, on a computer, or on a notepad—as long as you are able to get your thoughts on paper and able to go back to read what you have written. You could even speak your thoughts into a tape recorder and transcribe them later. Subscribe to a magazine about writing. Read the articles to learn what others have done. Discover new ways to plan your time and organize your plot lines. Invest in a vocabulary builder, a dictionary, and a thesaurus. Play games with your friends where you identify a word of the day or use a new, similar word to replace a common word you always use. Now, you are on your way to achieving the vision of being a writer. After all, you are doing the things that a writer does. Continue to produce. Self-fulfilling prophecy... Faith is as real as your will to live that reality.

The End of Wanting

Too often, you look at the success as the finished product of the producer. You conclude that you cannot achieve the same success. You fail to see the time, the habits of mind, the schedule, and the discipline the producer put into achieving her wish. You only see the end result. If you do glimpse what it takes to achieve, you are overwhelmed. Take heart! Though the process seems overwhelming, it is a process. This means that the beginning of a complicated success begins with that first simple action.

Be sure that you are planning actions based on an honest view of the habits of the producers that you would like to emulate. Recognize that producers rarely are able to articulate what they have done in order to achieve success. They sometimes inflate the time or romanticize the actions they performed on the way to their goals. They either over estimate or dismiss the help they received from others.

For example, the producer, when asked how he achieved, may say, "You have to work hard each day and read a lot." When asked if that was his process, the producer admits, "Oh, no. I don't really read that much." If you could have been a fly on the wall throughout the producer's process, you would have observed a process of idea formulation and commitment to product that spanned multiple years. Even the producer is not aware of how each choice, each rehearsal, each class, was a contribution toward the final product. The producer does not intentionally mislead with his responses, but the achievement of success sometimes reframes the journey as a function of destiny rather than a result of determination.

Understand that all sustainable success—the end of wanting— is the result of your determination over time to work, to lead with purpose, to incorporate new knowledge and relationships, and to risk being wrong. Maintain those habits. Connect those dots until patterns emerge and habits result in products.

SECTION II: DISTRACTIONS

Distractions: institutionalized representations of collective deception.

CHAPTER 5
DISTRACTIONS: BARRIERS TO AGENCY

Distraction occurs when you are preoccupied with something other than the dissonance that motivates your progress. The intensity required for learning and behavior change is not achieved. These manifest as unsustainable sociocybernetic effects—social contracts that enforce conformity, satisfaction with the status quo, and make it "strange" and unacceptable to suggest a different truth.

Social Contracts and Political Correctness

Up to this point, I have focused on describing your options as an individual. You have often been deceived. You have also been distracted. Institutions have standardized your deception allowing you to hide behind the plausible deniability of corporate conformity. The more clearly you understand your own identity, the more inconsistent the world appears. This may tempt you to give up on agentic success—achievement conceived by self-reflectiveness, self-reactiveness, intentionality, and forethought. But, take heart. We can overcome the distractions.

Institutions maintain your deception by distracting you from addressing your lack of sustainability. Instead of figuring out why a choice did not work out as you had hoped, you are lulled into a sense of comfort with disappointment, surrounded by people who support this passivity.

If only you would look within yourself. Reflect on your goals, your actions, your reasoning. Determine the origins for your choices. Evaluate your will to succeed. The institutions suggest that to focus on you is to deny community. Yet, this supposed altruism is not consistent with the other messages the institution espouses.

You are told to measure your success by your consumption—if you are the best, you must have the best. You are told to conform so as not to stick out from the crowd—it is conceit to proclaim your giftedness and heresy to pursue an alternative inquiry. You are told to apologize as a reflex in order to avoid conflict—it is better not to make enemies of people you do not know. Standards are relaxed in order to save the feelings of the mediocre.

Consumerism is the institutional method to medicate through entertainment and recreation. But, you think it is the frivolity that weakens the production focus. It is not the activity that is the problem. The problem is that you are not clear about your contribution. You risk shutting me out because you cannot see the opportunity for our collaboration.

Shame is the institutional tool that seeks to deny individual giftedness in favor of the collective identity. The expressed goals are to maintain order, to be fair, and lend predictability to chaos. To bow, conforming to shame is to stunt the chaos that motivates change and inspires growth in you and in me.

Guilt is the institutional source of choices that attempt to fix past failures. Rather than achieve goals based in principle, the guilt reflex suggests that you apologize because the goals may offend the sensibilities of another. The distraction is the quest for politeness, rather than the insistence on excellence. In this way, clear communication gives way to political correctness.

Human Nature: Balance, Morals & Adulthood

Balance

Fritz Heider has been credited with illuminating a most fundamental human trait, called Balance theory. The power of the human mind is demonstrated in that you can convince yourself of anything. You are motivated to create balance in your opinions about objects in the world around you. You form opinions about objects like people, places, your favorite novel, a style of car, your ability, and more. Objects are sometimes related. The challenge we must face together is that the relationships between the objects can cause you dissonance. A further challenge, you will typically resolve your dissonance in whichever way requires the least amount of effort. When faced with dissonance, Heider suggests that you will either:

a) Change your opinion of the original object
b) Change your opinion of the object being related, or
c) Deny that the relationship between objects exists.

Each of the options above is based on two fallacies. The first fallacy is that you have to make a decision as quickly as possible to regain balance using only the information that you currently have on hand. I offer to you that you must learn to tolerate ambiguity. You must seek knowledge that provides you with multiple views of objects and the relationships between them. The time it takes to seek out this new knowledge is not wasted time. Taking time to inform you could mean the difference between a sustainable balance that makes room for growth and an unsustainable balance that stifles growth.

The second fallacy is that the stress of dissonance is an enemy to health and wellbeing. You must put in the work required to decide the solution to dissonance that is best for you, and best for our collaboration. The stress brought about by the feeling of dissonance can be the motivation you need to consider new alternatives, seek new knowledge, and part with "easy" answers.

For example, you believe that you are a capable writer, and you have submitted a draft of a paper that we are working on together. I respond to your draft with a number of edits and corrections. In response to this you could choose to:

a) Decide that you are not a capable writer
b) Conclude that I am not a good collaborator, or
c) Conclude that writing is not an important skill.

Another option exists as well. Consider that you have more to learn about the type of writing that forms the basis of our collaboration. Also, consider that my edits are not a critique of your writing, but my contribution to our eventual product. Now, the question is more precisely, are you motivated to engage in the knowledge seeking required to learn more about writing, or will you give up on the collaboration?

The stress of the dissonance is the motivator. You know this in your thought, "I don't agree with your edits. Why did you write it that way?" Now, find out. Let us discuss our collaborative work. Let us agree on a definitive source or group of sources for our pattern for writing. Our collaboration is not your search for balance. Our interaction will challenge both of us to rethink our pre-collaboration givens, to create knowledge through our collective process—beyond the expertise of one individual.

Moral Attitudes

Our values are shaped by the experiences and opportunities we perceive.

Judson Mills (1958) conducted a study of sixth graders assessing their moral attitudes following temptation. Social scientists reading this text will be interested to know that Mills' advisor was Leon Festinger (!). The study offered differing rewards to students after they were tempted to cheat. It then asked them how they felt about others who cheat.

In the study, groups of students who cheated and received a big prize and students who did not cheat and received a small prize had no change in moral attitudes. Those who did cheat and received a small prize displayed a more lenient attitude toward cheating. Those who did not cheat and received a big prize evidenced a more severe attitude toward cheating.

The results suggest that, your attitudes are shaped by the experiences, opportunities, and rewards you perceive. The central question concerns values. Let us separate values from moral attitudes. In the Mills study above, recognize the two variables that call the results into question.

First, who told you that an opportunity to perform must be considered an opportunity to cheat or not to cheat? Second, who determined for you that one prize was bigger and therefore, more desirable than another? These two questions are questions about what you value—your individualized assessment of what is important in any given situation. My point: the value of morality is the relationship above all. Ask yourself whether the moral question supports relationship sustainably. Actions that do not violate valued relationships are potentially viable options no matter how others may frown upon them.

Let's work through an example. A college student, enrolled in a Calculus course, worked to complete a take-home examination. Upon handing out the exam, the instructor for the course specifically reminded the students that the examinations should be independent work. Our college student heard this as, "Don't cheat."

The student was playing computer games in a friend's dorm room the next day. Six other students from the class were sitting around and talking about the take-home exam as one student worked on his exam. They asked questions about his technique, formulas, and logic. Periodically, one student or another, would leave the dorm room for minutes, and return to the conversation afterward. Our student thought nothing of it at the time, and continued to play video games.

Graded examinations were distributed a week after the examination was due. Our student received a 70/100. The six other students' scores were all above 80% with no two scores the same. Our student realized that those students had an advantage. You need to understand that the advantage the other students possessed was not cheating, it was collaboration.

Consider your perceptions. First, do not reduce an opportunity to perform to a simple choice to cheat or not to cheat. An opportunity to perform is an opportunity for learning. Regardless of the reward, how best can you learn the lessons of this current opportunity? What resources do you have at your disposal? Will your use of those resources violate relationship?

What the six students did was study together. They learned from each other. They created community. They, then, dispersed to complete their exams with that collective knowledge. Our student, just as you seem to, worked on his examination alone. Alone.

Second, ask yourself whether our student learned anything of value. Of course, 70 is a lower score than 80. But, those scores only apply to the course. The real deficiency for our student is that he may never learn the lesson of community. He may never learn that scores are not evaluations of worth, they are measures of your engagement and potentially an indication of a need to ask for help and new information.

If you can move beyond the material, the temporal, the right-now, and the external, you will win. If you can define success for yourself in the context of community, you will succeed. If you can value the movement, celebrate the small successes, and collaborate, you will change your world. Our student learned what you must learn. Morality is worthless if it does not promote sustainable relationship and the identification of collective activities.

Adulthood

No doubt you have seen the caricatures of the stoic, no-nonsense, all-about-business adult who reconnects with his inner child. The comedy of the movie may be exaggerated, but the character is real. You have grown up with that seeming insistence that childish things be put aside for adult responsibilities. You may have even admonished others to, "Grow up!"

In saying these words, you were trying to make a distinction between the frivolity of youth and the responsibility of adulthood. You categorize many of the activities of your youth as childish and therefore beneath your adult station. Coloring, bike riding on your street, playing with toys, building forts with blankets, video games, and cartoons are now off limits.

Be clear. Adulthood requires maturity. But, no growth process is sustainable if later processes do not build on prior processes. One of the most important conceptions when recovering from trauma experienced during childhood is the acknowledgement of your inner child. Often, recovery is supported by rediscovering the joy that was interrupted in childhood. This rediscovery does not thwart adulthood and produce childishness evidenced in a lack of personal responsibility. For you, though, understanding the process of recovery may require a clearer definition of maturity. Even if you do not feel that you experienced trauma as a child, sustainable adulthood must build upon childhood.

Maturity is the recognition that your pursuits, your choices, have consequences not only for you, but for others as well. Play. Eat dessert first. Love shamelessly. Forgive quickly, and collaborate. And also, seek new knowledge, respond with a larger vision of the world, accept the responsibility, and wisely wield the power of adulthood. Growing up does not mean damping the lamp of childhood. Nurture that flame to burn as a legacy to your children's children—and an ever-present vigil to your children's inner child.

CHAPTER 6
CONSUMERISM

Consumerism describes your choice to medicate through entertainment and recreation. But, you think it is the frivolity that weakens the production focus. It is not the activity that is the problem. The problem is that you are not clear about your contribution. You risk shutting me out because you cannot see the opportunity for our collaboration. You shut me out because you do not realize your contribution to our relationship.

Distractions Case Study: 1 of 3

Our story from an ancient text continues. Remember that our main characters, Adam and Eve, were attendants to a beautiful garden. Eve entered into a conversation that served her ambitions well, but it was a conversation that left her and Adam confused. They both lived in this garden, content with themselves and the garden except for an insistent desire for knowledge. The text emphasizes that both were naked and felt no shame.

We pick up the story as Adam and Eve have consumed fruit from the tree that they were forbidden to touch. The primary result of their consumption is hidden. Of interest is the immediate loss of that sense of contentment with themselves. They became aware that they were naked. Contentment was replaced with a constant nagging, a feeling that something was missing sparked by the emptiness of what they had consumed. From that moment on, Adam and Eve craved recreation hoping to satiate that longing for completeness.

The greater loss was their desire for knowledge. The need for recreation now took priority. As the word re-creation suggests, they desired to be new—to experience the covering of their creator as they had when they took their first breath. They longed for that experience back when knowledge was the most important of their pursuits. They were now lost, and knowledge—the lessons of each experience— were less important. Their priority was to recover their original purity.

Consumers buy what's sold.
Producers create what's needed.

Whether you accept the story as truth or not, the truth is that you too have the longing. But, as with much in this life, the longing is not the problem. What you do to fill the longing, though, could be problematic. You attempt to satiate the longing with amusement, but you quickly realize that amusement does not equal contentment. The need is not simple recreation, but re-creation—renewal of your motivation to produce, feeding of your giftedness, and commitment to contribute your best self to community. But, the challenge is far more complex because you have lost your ability to engage authentically in the pursuit of your goals. You have not nurtured your capacity for learning. You want your best without work, without failure, and without resistance. You want it as simple as taking a pill or biting a piece of fruit. And, you have forgotten knowledge. Now, you are only focused on the outcome of knowledge. You have become a consumer only. Where once you had the capacity for balance between consumption and production, you now consider the consumption as somehow validation of self without a need for the evidence that results from producing. In other words, you think that *having things* means that you are successful, rather than honoring the *work and learning* as success. You want to HAVE success, not BE success.

Destination Preoccupation

You have been misled. You believe that the point is to arrive. Not true. The point is to walk within your ability, to govern yourself, and to influence the world around you. Success is a daily peak experience and contribution. It has been said that action speaks louder than words. Your life is a message for all who are listening. Each choice you make speaks another volume. Even when your life is over, consider that your legacy endures.

Destination preoccupation is the distraction of seeing your goals as a destination to arrive at rather than a role and responsibility to fulfill. This distraction creates an arbitrary limit to creativity. It allows you stop the process of development because you have arrived. When success is about making money or making the grade, you can stop producing when you make the money or make the grade. When success is about being your best, you never lose the motivation to make your honest and best contribution.

Think about the goals you now hold. Ask yourself, what you will do when you have reached those goals. Envision what those achievements make possible. If you cannot see beyond the successes you envision, you may be limiting your creativity. Creativity, in this way, is like water. It is bounded by the container it is placed within. If your container limits you to $100,000, your creativity will only expand to reach those levels. If your container limits to a 4 bedroom house, you have effectively limited your creativity. But, those are things. If your container makes other containers possible through its being a container, your contribution continues as long as you have a container.

The solution, therefore, is not to expand your success to larger monetary denominations or bigger houses. The solution is in reviewing your role and responsibility within the community you wish to impact. The responsibility starts with your family and those you want to help and support. Envision what level of success and attending materials are required to conduct your role responsibly. Success is less about how much you want to make, and more about how much you need to deliver on your role and responsibility. Adjust your vision of success in step with your level of responsibility. In this way, the greater and more far reaching your desired success, the greater and more far reaching is your eventual responsibility.

Revision of Destination Preoccupation

A revision of success along the lines of individual role and responsibility to the community forces less attention to destination and more attention to process. It is a realization that the accolades and achievements of wealth and status are secondary to the learning and community created in the process. When you are working toward individual and community success, you never arrive at a final destination. You are always building toward greater success. You are also expanding your influence with each step and incurring more responsibility. It is a process of becoming in each moment.

Consider the goal of being an author. It is not the book signing, the 3-picture movie deal, or the translation into 30 languages that defines the author. It is the writer who writes with a passion, discipline, and consistency. Destinations make for headlines, but do not be fooled. Destinations are defined by the road leading up to them. Any moment along the way, you can be distracted. With the distraction comes at least a delaying of your becoming and a change in your being. At worst, distraction derails your vision and redefines who you are. Attend with eyes wide open to the current step only looking forward to the next step.

Re-creation

I propose that you have the desire to know and to create. A proposition because you have been told that you need to change. Your sustainable development is not about change. It is about integration. It is not about your wrongness and need for correction. It is about your ignorance concerning the options available to you.

Your desire for knowledge and will to create is strong enough that, if not met with opportunity to produce, you act out in ways that an observer may perceive as irrational and even self-destructive. Truth is, much of what you would apologize for or feel shame about were moments in which your boredom with everyday consumption motivated you to reach for something new without regard for whether it was sustainable or not. My purpose is to explain that it was not simply a moment of weakness. It was the result of a pattern of unsustainable choices and consumption leading logically to an undesired outcome. You were set up...by yourself.

You search for peak experiences. The solution is to create mechanisms to arrive at those peak experiences through sustainable means. You have options. You can integrate all of who you are. Enjoy sustainable selfishness. Produce even in your leisure. Find balance in work and play as less dissimilar and as more of a lifestyle of peak experiences.

CHOOSE PRODUCTIVE ENVIRONMENTS

Certain environments increase the chance for unsustainable choices. For example, the night club is much better with alcohol or the promise of sex. Alcohol releases you from your inhibitions, because it impairs your judgment. It engages your pleasure sense—a result of the slowing of mental response time and lack of ability to focus. You effectively shut down your ego and superego and live out the fantasies of your id. This means that your instincts take control of your behavior. Your hidden desires are more likely to manifest in your behavior. When you find that you have acted inappropriately and made unsustainable choices, it should be no surprise. You were set up...by yourself.

The alcohol is not the problem. As with Adam and Eve in our case study, it was not the mere existence of alcohol that precipitated its consumption. It was your proximity to the alcohol. Your first step toward re-creation that supports production is to **choose environments where the enhancers are consistent with sustainable choices**. Why choose the night club, alcohol, late night, no responsibilities, no morning appointments, an invited night cap, and that person who you know enough to allow opportunity? You could choose an evening meal, dancing, good nights, a cab ride, and a restful sleep.

You need to be concerned about each of the choices as they are made. If you choose club, alcohol is not the most sustainable choice to add. If you do choose alcohol, next choosing late night takes you further from your goals. My point is not that you chose club as a "wrong" choice. It is that you continued along a predictable pattern toward unsustainable choices and unintended outcomes without being aware that you could have redirected the prediction through different choices.

INTEGRATE YOUR PERSON

This step is illustrated in the dichotomy of integrating versus apologizing. You can apologize for something you have done, but never apologize for who you are. Know your demons and your desires. **Meet your desires with sustainable choices**. Stop telling yourself that your desires are bad. It is your choices that should concern you. Want is not the problem. Acting unsustainably on desires can be your undoing. Consider that you can meet your desires in sustainable ways.

It does not matter to your health that you love to eat. It matters that you create a lifestyle that allows for indulgent eating AND health. Just as Inuit peoples living among snow will have multiple words for the frozen precipitation, you will have many words for tasting, sampling, eating, indulging, and gorging on food to distinguish the level of partaking in a meal. Integration suggests that you will also have corresponding words for the level of physical activity and body detox required for partaking in your favorite pastime. Rather than allow someone to place in your head the idea that what you desire is unhealthy, self-indulgent, or wrong, create a means to integrate your desires into a lifestyle that works for you while maintaining progress toward your goals of health, wealth, and wisdom.

ENJOY SUSTAINABLE SELFISHNESS

The instructions for loss of cabin pressure on an airplane suggest that you should place your mask on prior to helping any other passenger with his mask. This is a selfish approach to this situation. Sure! But, this procedure ensures that you can remain conscious while attempting to help someone else.

You tend toward self-protection and safety. Stop apologizing for this, and begin to integrate this part of your personality into your evaluation of self and your choices. The value of your approach ensures that you remain in a position to produce and even to support others. Now, rather than lamenting your personality as a hindrance, choose what you will produce and how you will contribute. Rather than "trying to be nice," communicate intentionally with honesty and respect. You will intimidate some, ruffle some feathers, and turn away some casual connections. But, you will also make connections that are authentic, long-lasting, and purposeful.

RECREATE PRODUCTIVELY

I submit to you that you have never stood alongside another honoree after having produced and thought, "This is not such a big deal." But, there are many times when you have watched from the bleachers or the couch and silently thought, "I could have done that." Your need to produce is the root of your frustration.

In order to fully appreciate the contribution of others, you must produce. **Ensure that you know where your recreation fits into your production cycle.** Another way to say this is "feed your giftedness." When faced with options for your recreation, consider how the activity informs you. Take the time to explore the relationship between the activity and your production goals. Choose activities that provide just the right balance of relaxation and alertness. This is fertile ground for inspiration. Especially after intense work on a project, leisure activity along with reflection can fill in blanks, complete thoughts, and answer questions.

For example, if you are a writer, watching movies could be a great way to recreate. Some would argue that reading is better, but you are not in the research or training mode during recreation. You are allowing your mind to wander and make connections as it will. Choose what feels like recreation to you. You know whether your choice was sustainable or not by evaluating whether your motivation was recharged or frustrated. Recharge or inspiration is the goal. Frustration suggests that the activity be crossed off the list of options. With practice, your recreation will actually fuel your productivity.

Balance the work and the play. Do not be intimidated by the work. More work means more time for the types of recreation that are needed for inspiration. Realize that, as Rollo May has proposed, creativity is both form and art. Inspiration is found in those moments of reflection and fun after those moments of intense thought and work.

LOOK BEHIND THE HIGHLIGHT REELS

Remove your tendency toward comparison. Stand firm in the knowledge that your gift will make room for you. Your success is uniquely yours to achieve. Your production will reflect your unique perception of the need and your specific connection to a target population.

When you see someone's finished product, you are often seeing the result of investment over a long period of time. When you get to your work bench, it appears that you are not working at the same pace as your peers. Without even comparing the resources, experiences, or supports the other has present, realize that you are only seeing the results. You are not privy to the percolations of inspiration, the anxiety of anticipation, and the sleepless nights of production. You need only **focus on the assurance that your continued work will yield a finished product**.

Just think, products take time. One of the hardest things to do is to complete a project, and then proofread or quality check it yourself. Realize that quality check is only one part of the project when you are starting out. After the proofread, you have to package. After packaging, you have to promote. After promotion, you have to evaluate, make changes, control branding, and follow-up with interactions. All this, and you should be working on your next product. It is difficult and complex. My point to you is that it is common. Realize that others, even those models of success that you look up to, had to put in this time.

Most people started out with just a dream. Some with a dollar and a dream. Some had backing and a wealth of mentors. Even then, they had to make the choice to listen. Every support and allowance for support that you have adds value and shortens the time to production. But, nothing is automatic. Resist the anxiety that comes from watching someone else's highlight reel. Three minutes of highlights are the result of hours of video.

CHAPTER 7
COMMUNITY OF SHAME

Shame is the impulse to run and hide in the face of truth. In groups, shame can be utilized to deny individual giftedness in favor of the collective identity. The expressed goals are to maintain order, to be fair, and lend predictability to chaos. To bow, conforming to shame, is to stunt the chaos that motivates change and inspires growth in you and in me.

Distractions Case Study: 2 of 3

Their eyes were opened, and they realized they were naked. They sewed fig leaves together to cover themselves.

Returning to our story from the ancient text... At this point in the story, Adam and Eve have eaten from the tree they were forbidden to touch. In the moment that they ate from the tree, they realized that they were naked. Their next thought was, "We have to cover ourselves." Our two characters gathered fig leaves, and sewed them together to make coverings.

The creator again visited the garden hoping to engage with the man and woman that he created. He was surprised to find that they were hidden. He knew something was wrong. He called out to Adam, his first creation, "Where are you?"

Notice what happened next. Adam did not respond with his location. He immediately explained his guilt. "I heard you in the garden, and I was afraid because I was naked. Logically, I hid."

Adam and Eve made a grave mistake, and they immediately felt ashamed. You too have made mistakes, and immediately felt ashamed. The reflex is to cover your shame and hide it as if it did not happen. The problem is that this reflex becomes a pattern feeding into your instinct for self-protection used whenever you are threatened and whenever you are faced with something that you are not familiar with. And thus, the cycle of stunted growth is initiated.

It does not matter whether the opportunity is sustainable or unsustainable. You do not possess any objective criteria for evaluating the difference. You have secrets that you dare not expose. You choose to err on the side of caution rather than risk exposure. You conform with others who promise to keep questions to a minimum. You silence yourself, the real you, to the point that you do not know who YOU are anymore. You isolate yourself, which only serves to stagnate your learning. You never learn the reward that results from moving outside of your protective zone because you never risk.

I want you to wear your individual giftedness as unashamed nakedness. You must engage uncovered in our relationship. Call shame by name, and remove its power to silence you. Inspire you and me by being your best self.

The goal should be to identify what your contribution will be to our team. It really does not matter what activity you engage in.

When you are clear about your contribution, you see value, gain knowledge, and notice complexities in what others may see as frivolous. Your inadequacies, lack of knowledge, inabilities, and deficits are not disqualifications. In community, you are only responsible for your contribution. You are only called to do what you can do. If we each perform at a high level that which we are slated to do, the community will have all that it needs through our collective action.

Shame & Your Moral Compass (Objective Criteria)

Truth may manifest in the form of trauma you experience, increased awareness, mistakes you make, or inconsistencies within your environment. The problem is that the uncertainty of the new tends to support your recoil reaction toward safety. You make this choice even though it diminishes options, long-term coping, and future learning. When your reaction is the result of trauma—pain, negative experiences, or intense longing—diminished neurodevelopment can result, especially in the case of childhood trauma. The further effects may include diminished capacity.

You begin to feel that you cannot trust yourself or your gift. You lose the sense of a moral compass with a true North. You begin to rely on external guides ignoring your internal voice and sense of individual contribution. Any option—outside of what is forbidden by your permissive peer group, what lingers after your self-medication, what convinces beyond your capacity to reason, and what fits your immediate environment—will make sense. You adopt options even when they are unsustainable.

Your continued dissonance in attempting to reconcile your continued failure to make sustainable choices forces you to practice the tools of shame: silence as denial, conformity as a form of deceit, and isolation as self-protection. This practice leaves you stagnated, your potential unrealized, your success delayed.

Your task is to create **objective criteria** for distinguishing the difference between a sustainable choice and an unsustainable choice. Objective criteria are not based in the shame that forces you into silence, conformity, isolation, and stagnation. You will know objective criteria—a sustainable moral compass—because you will feel a power born out of responsibility, coping centered in your giftedness, the challenge of positive competition from a supportive peer group, and an openness revealing your motives and actions as identical.

Power over Silence

Silence is more than just quiet. It is also the way you slink away in the face of shame. The problem is your denial of your trauma. This is the power of shame. Shame is silent about its source. If you shared a thousand words without speaking the evil of your trauma, your words will never bring you satisfaction. If you work a thousand hours toward your survival without acknowledging the source of your fear, you will never feel safe. If you reclaim a relationship without discussing the hurt that you suffered, you will never be healed. The relationship is a shell of form and function without spirit and life.

Call shame out. Never be afraid to voice your trauma, your fear, your hurt. Your endeavors to recover will have more effect when they target the offending source directly. If you are speaking to respond to those who said you do not have a voice, speak that truth. If you are working to never face the poverty of your life growing up, acknowledge that motivation. If you are reconnecting with an estranged father to inform him of the loss you feel from his absence in your life, discuss that memory.

A sustainable redress of trauma is grounded in self-development. Your confrontation of the trauma is not about feeding your energy to the trauma. The confrontation is about releasing yourself from the timeline and decision tree of trauma. It is a proclamation that your energy will be used to seek out new and alternative options beyond the anemic offerings thrust upon you by trauma responses. The confrontation is a commitment to write yourself a new back story of resilience as opposed to victimization. **This is your power**—the realization that your ability to make this next choice is evidence of your victory over the past. Develop that power into a confidence and expectation that you can overcome any challenge in the future as well.

Giftedness over Conformity

In an attempt to identify an external North on your moral compass, you deny individualism and collectivism at the same time. Because it did not work to look out for yourself, you cannot trust that your gift will make room for you. Because you lost yourself in the crowd of cliché answers, victimization, and facelessness, you cannot trust that a community exists that will welcome you—all of you...the real you. The problem is that your decision to conform removes your individual responsibility for your choices. You have an out by saying, "I was doing what they told me to do." You can disregard the power that you have to make your own choices. You can disregard the impact of your choices on the world around you. Most distressing, you obscure your individual gift. All the while, you are in a protective cocoon of followers—a group known by one name, faceless, and marked by plausible deniability. You cannot be seen as one. You cannot be accused separate from the whole.

You must get back to the motivation that connected directly to your gift and idea. At some point early on in your experience, you believed that you could do better than simple coping. You understood that you could create the beauty you wanted to see in the world and inspire others to do the same. It will take time because the path to your success has obstacles. It will seem lonely, and you will often feel like you are out on a limb. But each result, each feeling, reminds you of the frailty of a new endeavor and motivates you to develop further with new relationships, new information, and new role definitions. Such is work, but consider the reward.

The expression of your giftedness creates community. The definition of new relationships is a network of others you may motivate, inspire, and partner with. This network expands your reach, and shares support reciprocally. New information informs both your gift and your reach. You learn as a result of both achievements and disappointments. You increase in knowledge optimizing your individual intelligence, developing your individual genius. New role definitions allow you to structure new worlds of collaboration and collective action. You allow yourself and others to extend beyond the expected and the trite. You connect with others in new ways without the restraints of power-based, hierarchical, and paternalistic views of leadership and followership.

Reciprocity over Isolation

Shame suggests to you that no one can be trusted to know, respect, and appreciate you for who you are unless they are as broken as you appear. As a result, you make judgments about relationships based on your assessment of whether or not you have the upper hand. You think you are the master, in control of the relationships you have. You shy away from relationships in which you cannot see a clear advantage.

The problem with your prior relationships was not necessarily the power differential between you and the other. The problem was that the currency was not agreed upon. Determine sustainable relationships by discussing what will be expected from you and what you will receive in return. Ask the same from the other. Learn that you are not required to give everything in every relationship. Healthy relationships involve give and take from all parties involved. You decide what contributions are comfortable for you and what receipts are expected from the other.

You must **master reciprocity. Make it your reciprocity.** Your reciprocity moves reciprocity from being a simple practice to being a contract, an evaluation, and a means of maintenance. A contract because your reciprocity requires firm, intentionally stated commitment. An evaluation because your reciprocity reveals the flaws of others who are fearful of or resistant to engagement in a formal contract. Your reciprocity is a means of maintenance because it outlines the give and take that defines each relationship for the long-term. There is no shame in termination of the contract. There is only joy in the value gained from your reciprocity.

Transparency over Stagnation

In the midst of choices motivated by shame, it makes perfect sense to hide your ideas and progress, your intentions and feelings, your whereabouts and plans under the banner of "privacy." But, where did you learn that there is a distinction between the giving of yourself and your desired success? I am not suggesting that you throw caution to the wind and make your location known through minute-by-minute posts to social media. I am suggesting that you develop a window into your work and development specifically targeting the population that will benefit and appreciate your contribution. I am suggesting that you realize the value and use of a supportive network. In this suggestion, I am sharing the bias that your life is about the influence you make. There can be no success in obtaining without sharing.

Even better than a window, would be a mechanism for dialogue between you and your potential market for influence. Engage with others to test your solutions against the real problems they face. Experience the rejection and questions of security that can accompany the sharing of your work with others. From that experience, gain insight into the unspoken needs of others, and the reserves of curiosity, resilience, and drive that you have within yourself. Learn that it is important, not shameful, for your work to be criticized.

Your transparency is about revealing your truth, but it is driven by the purpose of influencing curiosity, resilience, and drive in others. This will certainly result in the same for you. Curiosity manifests in the search for meaning surrounding your achievements and apparent failures. Resilience is illustrated in your ability to bounce back and engage authentically with an expectation of conversation. Drive is revealed in that insistence on perseverance that is not a "have to do" but a "who I am" approach to the tasks of each day. You do what you do, not because you have to, but because it is who you are.

Accountability is Not Shame

As a coach and as a friend, my goal is to be ME unapologetically and always encouraging YOU to do the same. It is always enlightening when I get glimpses of how my ME is perceived by others. It was a conversation with a student that prompted my reflection on my influence.

STUDENT: I was having lunch the other day, telling my friend stories about my life. She told me that I have so much to write, and I need to write a book. I thought, "Don't let Dr. Wright hear you say that."

ME: Why not? All I'm going to do is encourage you to do it.

As I contemplated the conversation continuing my exploration of motivation, I hit on a familiar set of distractions that plague individuals and frustrate productive relationships. I present them to you because they threaten to limit your development and thereby limit our collective action. I will begin by stating the truth. First, guilt and shame are different. Second, even healthy relationships often incur guilt as primordial motivation. Third, your prioritization of value determines whether you respond productively to the conviction of guilt.

Distinguishing Guilt and Shame

With every experience of falling short of a goal, you are faced with guilt that has the potential to metastasize into shame. Simply put, guilt is active, taking responsibility. Shame is passive, having blame assigned to you. Guilt causes you to assess what you have done wrong, and take steps to correct your behaviors. Shame causes you to seek cover. If you do not like conflict, you hide with denial and avoidance. If you are more comfortable with conflict, you engage attempting to refocus the light of conviction on something other than your behaviors and your choices.

When you have fallen short, determine whether you are responding to guilt or to shame. If you are responding to guilt you will ask, "What choices did I make that were not in line with my goals? What choices can I make now to move sustainably toward my goals?" In shame while avoiding conflict, you will isolate yourself, stop answering calls, and limit engagement. If you are responding to shame engaging conflict, you will exclaim, "There are many reasons why I am not achieving my goals! Few people understand my struggle." The problem with shame is that it obscures the desired goals in favor of self-protection or saving-face goals. Energy that could be used to satisfy curiosity, resilience, and motivation is siphoned off for resistance, excuses, and rationalization. Take responsibility and reclaim that energy in order to try again, better informed, with greater support, and increased endurance.

Social Control and Relationships

Four types of social control exist. Direct social control forces you to do what is required. Internal social control is influence on choice centered in your conscience or sense of right and wrong. Indirect social control influences your choices through relationships. Needs satisfaction is a means of social control that seeks to provide for all your possible needs with the expectation that you would then act in accordance with what is required.

I want to focus on INDIRECT social control in our exploration of shame. In this type, the relationship influences choice behavior. You want to do "good" in order to honor the relationship you have with another person.

For example, you want to finish your college degree to honor your grandmother. You do not necessarily WANT to study or write papers, but you are motivated to complete these. Completion means passing grades, which means graduation, which means honor for your grandmother. It would be great if you developed intrinsic motivation and wanted to achieve for yourself. It would be exceptional if you developed an interest and aspired to research and contribute to the knowledge base of a profession. But, it is enough that you are motivated even at the most fundamental level.

The challenge of shame is apparent when you fail a course. You can respond with guilt or shame. Guilt causes you to find tutoring and address your study habits. Shame causes you to blame teachers or the system. My point is that your grandmother still loves you and has not changed her support. Yet, you feel that you have let her down in some small way. Relationships incur guilt. Because you value the relationship, you are motivated to respond. Your chosen response to the situation has implications for your ability to meet the next challenge. Again, your grandmother's love has not changed.

The problem is not your relationship with your grandmother. The conviction is YOURS, and so is the choice. The conviction that comes with guilt motivates action. You can constructively respond to guilt before it becomes shame. Guilt can be a welcomed motivator and an indication that you need to seek help or more information. Use it to develop a strategy for overcoming the obstacle.

Replace mentor, teacher, friend, spouse or other supports where "grandmother" is in the example above. The relationship and the guilt are not the problems. They are the motivation. If shame enters the picture, you will begin to see blame where you once saw support. Embrace guilt motivating a search for additional resources as readily as you embrace your support system.

Priorities in Your Response

Accountability is not shame. Accountability results in your feeling of guilt when a target is not met. What is critical to understand is stated in cliché, "Actions speak louder than words." Your choice tells all observers what you value. But, more than that, understand that to allow the insidiousness of shame diminishes your ability to self-correct and reach your goals. You in effect state through action, "It is more important to APPEAR driven than to drive myself toward my goals." You value approximations and appearances, things that can be explained through redirection and rationalization. Your actions in service to shame state this clearly.

A proactive response to guilt empowers you to take responsibility. You can even seek help because you are able to identify some areas you may need help to improve. Many obstacles still exist, but you choose to value your PROGRESS and eventual goal above the appearance of sobriety or piety in this moment.

The "excuses" that no one wants to hear are shame and denial that offers no perceivable opportunity for redress. Those who have committed to support you want to hear that you have recognized where you need help, and you are choosing to engage in consistent help seeking and corrective activity. Resist the urge to consider the conviction of accountability as shame. Enjoy and self-correct from guilt. It indicates value in the relationship.

I hope you are convicted at the thought of ME as you contemplate your goals. I hope you are encouraged by the fact that someone believes in your promise, believes in you, and will hold you accountable to your vision. I hope you are also mindful that the conviction of ME comes with my active investment in your success— a commitment to inform your curiosity, foster your resilience, and inspire your intrinsic motivation.

CHAPTER 8
THE GUILT REFLEX

Guilt is the feeling of conviction that causes humans to realize that they have offended a relationship. The guilt reflex is the impulse to fix your offenses often acting without thought of the long-term consequences. In the absence of your ability to assuage the guilt, you seek to blame someone else for your failure. Moving beyond the guilt reflex is realizing that hurt feelings are only repaired over time. No immediate fixes exist.

Distractions Case Study: 3 of 3

At this point in our story, the creator is in the garden. Adam has just confessed the feeling of shame. Even though he and Eve had fashioned fig leaves into a covering, Adam still hid when he heard the creator in the garden. And the creator asked, "Who told you that you were naked? Did you eat from the tree that I told you not to eat from?"

Adam responded with an explanation that you may be familiar with. More important than his exact words is the fact that he attempted to remove the responsibility, the light of truth, the exposure to guilt from himself and place it squarely onto Eve. This is the guilt reflex. Adam missed the opportunity to learn from his mistake through accountability for its consequences. What you may not have realized is the subtle way that Adam attempted to both reconcile his need to supplant his parent and honor the parent's historical influence.

In his response, Adam revealed that he wanted to take on the mantle of protector and authority. He moved to fashion fig leaves. He hid. His explanation recognized the authority of the creator, and evidenced Adam's presumption that the creator would be offended at the site of the naked couple. In this, Adam demonstrated a natural process of age and adult development in which the child learns **autonomy**.

"The woman you gave me...," Adam's famous deflection of guilt, places the blame for the whole incident at the foot of the creator. By extension, Adam was lamenting the fact that the creator had even created the tree with the forbidden fruit. It was the tantrum of "I wish I was never born." It is a back-handed tribute to the power of the creator to make whatever **legacy** he sees fit.

You face the same two feats of choice as you mature into adulthood. You must learn autonomy—living separate from the control or influence of others. You must define your legacy—the enduring consequences of your choices made and your life lived.

Replace Adam with You. Replace the creator with your parents. Among other choices, you decide whether to prosecute your adulthood as an attempt to reclaim what you feel was lost during childhood, or to live autonomously creating honor for your parents and modeling honor to your children. What you are is an inevitability and your parent's fault if you want to see it that way. Autonomy is the choice to see that you make the choice of what you are and what you will become. Legacy is to focus on your responsibility to the future rather than expending energy to assign blame for the past.

The Success Equation: Autonomy, Parents, and Legacy

The research is clear. Your environment, relationships, and interactions from 0-18 years of age impact the rest of your life in profound, lasting ways. Adverse childhood experiences (ACEs) provide a list of the trauma experiences shown to correlate with unsustainable choice behavior and poor health outcomes. Multiple studies have supported the parental impact on child development. Google scholar lists 16,500 articles between 2010 and 2013 alone (google.com/scholar keyword: parental impact on child development). This, and my experience with clients, leads me to the following conclusion:

Everything that you are is a result of your struggle to solve the equation (both deficit and addition) you understand from your parents.

The challenge of every human is to solve this equation sustainably leaving a progressive legacy to their next generation. Even if your childhood was great, free from what you would consider to be trauma, do not assume that you have no equation. Everyone has a mission handed down to them from their parents. To refuse recognition of this influence risks missing the lessons that would support your sustainable success.

Formulating Your Equation

I offer a basic equation for comparison with your equation in order to illustrate the simplicity of the task and how it is complicated by parental impact. Consider that Success is achieved by giving your best. When you are attempting to compensate for a deficit or addition you perceive to be handed down from a parent, you modify the equation in ways that increase the complexity. Allow me to represent this in an equation:

Success = your B+E+S+T: **B**oundaries, **E**quifinality, **S**tructure of Transactions, **T**ransactions

"B" is for Boundaries. Your safety, well-being, and participation in the world around you can all co-exist. Your hesitance to trust others is uncertainty about self. You can construct rules that enable you to trust you.

"E" is for Equifinality. A multitude of relationships are possible connections to your success. Independence is not isolation. Success requires relationship. You can evaluate relationships discerning authenticity.

"S" stands for Structure of Transaction. Sustainable relationships are never one-sided. Build reciprocity into your interactions from the beginning. You can receive and give with expectation.

"T" stands for the Transactions themselves, the interactions with others. Engaging is the test, but it is also the lesson. Learn eagerly. You can wisely risk rejection and gain lessons that last.

Your B.E.S.T. is my mnemonic device to organize four important components of your generational narrative equation. The challenge with these four is that you have been misinformed about how they work in your equation. What is worse, you are often operating contrary to your BEST interests with the choices you make. Solutions are obscured by misinformation and polite society.

Your identification of the real challenge is clouded by **MISINFORMATION** received from your parents and others in your circle of influence. Understand that this misinformation resulted from their BEST efforts to deal with their own equations. Just as your success equation is shaped by your parents, their success equation was shaped by the generation before them. They communicated rules, discernment, structures, and protections that make sense to them.

My favorite example of this was replayed during a trip to the mall. I witnessed a mother repeatedly attempting to convince a 4 year old to say he was sorry for something he had done. "Say you're sorry!" she insisted as if convincing the child to vocalize the words somehow activated an inner sense of empathy for the suffering he had caused. This mother was certain that requiring her son to say the words was important enough to make a scene in the middle of a mall trip. Her son did not give in. Intrigued, I watched for a full 3 minutes as she repeated the command over and over again without the desired result.

The mother was enforcing what made sense to her, even if it made no sense to the child. Success for her in that moment was an empathetic child. She failed. My point is not her failure to coax an apology. My point is that her rules, discernment, structures, and protections did not account for the context or best practices in child rearing. Her method was a knee-jerk reaction in the mold she had seen modeled or used with her. She was misinformed.

Saying you are sorry does not mean that you have empathy. Being forced to say you are sorry is not effective in facilitating empathy. A discussion of feelings is required to develop empathy in a child. The child must realize the hurt caused, AND care about the hurt caused. You want autonomy and legacy. The child's resistance is actually evidence of your desired outcome. It is counter-intuitive to become a child development scholar in the face of being challenged by a 4 year old. Most parents believe that they can will a child to perform. But, the outcome desired is not mere performance.

Solutions to the challenges you face are obscured in much the same way. It seems counter-intuitive to stop, reflect, and learn before you react. Your natural instinct is to fix it the best you can right away. This is the guilt reflex. But, you don't want simple short-term fixes. You want emotional growth and maturity.

POLITE SOCIETY also provides a wealth of behaviors and context cue training. You are rewarded for your deference, playing small, pretentiousness, and risk aversion. This creates a culture of interaction that is devoid of honesty, authenticity, reciprocity, and learning.

My best examples of this are interviews given by many—I would venture to say most—successful people who give interviews. "Do you have any advice to anyone coming up in the industry?" they are often asked. Invariably, some version of the following answer is given, "Work hard, and never give up." This advice may make for a great bumper sticker, but it is a grand disservice to the question and an even bigger slap in the face to those who have worked diligently for years, and have not made significant progress.

If you want to know the real answer: It is just a truth that you may never reach your goals. The truth is horribly discouraging. But, from the foundation of this truth, you can build the vision, the network, the resources, and the work ethic that ensures a different reality. The hard work is more than just showing up with effort. It is enduring the uncertainty and the reality that you can do everything right and still not achieve certain goals. Never giving up is more than perseverance. It is a recognition that timing accounts for more of success than most are comfortable admitting. Success is relational from audience to supporters to customers. Your ability to connect an idea to a mature market at just the right time may result in your success. But, there is no guarantee.

Polite society obscures the virtue of honestly communicating the challenge. Authentic desire will find the opportunities within the challenge. Reciprocity will create the networks and mature them from supporters to customers. Learning gained in this process will pass intentionally to the next group of achievers.

Overcoming misinformation and polite society requires an approach to competence in each of the components of your success equation. Each offers you the chance to overcome the fallacy of dualism. You realize that you can choose both not just either. Achievements you once thought were at odds can actually become complementary. Each offers an opportunity for you to relearn. Each offers a challenge for you to solve sustainably. Yet, before you address the B.E.S.T., you must solve the results of the autonomy and legacy impact received from your parents. Autonomy challenges your need to live up to the expectations of your parents creating a sense of *deficit*. Legacy challenges you to produce beyond your parent's achievements concerned about your contribution—your *addition* to the family.

The guilt reflex is an attempt to compensate, without accounting for the *deficit/addition*. Let represent the *deficit/addition* with the word **Trauma**. Without this accounting, you change the calculus of the equation. You need to divide **Success** by the Trauma admitting that your need for autonomy and legacy alters the definition of your success.

$$\frac{Success}{Trauma} = \text{your B+E+S+T}$$

Yet, you refuse to do that because your sense of success is a truth that you hold believing that it should not be divided or otherwise altered. You turn, then, to redefining your B.E.S.T. in order to satisfy the equation. Your quest becomes a search for **satisfaction** instead of a **solution** to the equation. You are resigned to live in reaction rather than autonomy, and pass on a lesson of survival to be maintained rather than a legacy to build upon. The further regret is that your attempts to simple satisfaction WILL NOT support the success that you prize. This is because your compensation, the guilt reflex without solving for your B.E.S.T., results in choices that take you further from sustainable goal achievement.

In order to overcome the guilt reflex, you **have to let go** of the prized status of your Success truth. You have to allow the algebraic equation to be solved mathematically. You must divide Success by the Trauma you perceived from your parents. You make these adjustments all the time. My assertion is that your attempts without solving the Trauma are resignations as opposed to solutions (calculations).

The result of a conscientious, mathematical solution is a version of Success that is achievable in the context of your B.E.S.T. More importantly, once you are consonant with math versus conjecture, solution rather than satisfaction, legacy including the lessons, thriving beyond surviving, you can begin to change the equation. You can begin to multiply **Supports** toward your B.E.S.T., which increases your Success by cancelling out the Trauma handed to you by your experiences. The result is Success beyond what your parental impact and your B.E.S.T. supported alone. The more Supports you employ, the greater your amplification of your B.E.S.T., and the greater reduction in the impact of Trauma on Success. For example, you may not make your first million by the age of 30. But with Supports, you CAN re-calculate in order to achieve that milestone by age 45.

SOLUTION:

$$\text{Supports} * \frac{Success}{Trauma} = \text{your B+E+S+T} * \textbf{Supports}$$

RESULT:

$$\text{Success} = \text{your B+E+S+T} * \textbf{Supports}$$

THE PARENTAL OBLIGATION

The lessons of generations past are not to be neglected. You must inform your approach to your personal struggle.

Human interactions are not zero-sum propositions. One moment of hurt is not fixed by one moment of healing. If you lose a love opportunity, you cannot just replace it with another opportunity. Hurt cannot be made right as simply as solving an equation. The value placed on behaviors or experiences, the energy derived and expended, the motivation or lack thereof is not easily comprehended nor is it the same for each individual. Yet, this is not an unsustainable chaos. It is an opportunity to experience complexity as a motivator toward greater understanding. That quest for understanding is living.

You are guilty. That fact is not in dispute. The challenge is to resist the impulse to correct the situation NOW, without thinking. At best, you are unaware of unintended consequences. At worst, you make the situation worse for yourself and me. The impulse is to do something quickly. It does not matter if the action is sustainable, as long as it is quick. The problem is that this rush to action is not motivated by an attempt to salvage relationships. It is spurred by an attempt to save face. It is not motivated to heal, it is a swift bandage.

The difference between guilt and shame is that guilt motivates action. Shame paralyzes. Rarely, is the guilt-motivated action sustainable if not met with patience and wisdom. But, it is action just the same. Your task is to respond with intentionality to the conviction of guilt.

If you want to heal our relationship, you must accept blame and apologize. Your verbal apology is supported through your actions. Working together, we can outline action that will satisfy your debt and rebuild our shared trust. Understand that you cannot return to a time before the transgression occurred, but we can rebuild our relationship such that the transgression is not catastrophic.

Blame

Take a moment to think of other times you were guilty. You may have some lingering feelings of embarrassment. What if you had come clean right away when you hurt me? There is no question. You stepped on my foot. Will you commit to being more careful, or will you explain how the design of the aisles makes it impossible to miss stepping on a few feet?

Maybe the hardest thing to do when caught is to answer questions with a simple "yes" or "no." We learn in our youth that communicating context is important for influencing how we are judged. So, when asked if you are guilty, you attempt to provide the context of your transgression. You describe the situation, the players, the temptations, and the ambiance. You describe what you were "trying" to do and your "intentions."

What you fail to realize is that blame is power. I am less frustrated with your transgression. I am more disappointed that you explain yourself to be a puppet of circumstance and environment. If you cannot assume the power that accepting blame represents, I cannot trust you to make more sustainable decisions in the future. You are powerless to do so.

Imagine a relationship in which your perceived failures are known and immaterial. Imagine the sense of relief you would feel, to be imperfect yet responsible and intentional. Rather than the practice of shedding blame, accept blame to initiate your power to learn more about yourself and change the situation.

Practice discernment of the relationships that allow you to be yourself: Guilty sometimes, but always responsible and dedicated to improving. Nurture these relationships. At some point in time, I may be guilty. You may be guilty again. But, if we accept the blame, engaging each other intentionally, our relationship will grow in power and the ability to overcome our challenges.

Apology

Of course you should apologize. And, not the "I'm sorry" that some parents force from their offensive children. I am talking about an apology that acknowledges your wrong and the injury that you have caused. An adequate apology takes responsibility for the work that must be done now to systematically repair the relationship. To be truly repentant is to realize that you do not control the time it will take for forgiveness to replace pain.

The guilt reflex suggests that you apologize because you have offended the sensibilities of another. The distraction is the quest for politeness, rather than the quest for success. Clear communication gives way to political correctness. What you miss in the quest for politeness is the questioning and self-reflection that comes with injuring another person. You also reinforce a tendency to excuse rather than explain. Both politeness and excuse potentially stunt your growth individually and our growth relationally.

Rather than sweep it under the rug, let us explore your thought process and the choices you made to offend. This work can be difficult. You may say things that injure me again. But with conversation, comes the opportunity to respond, clarify, and challenge assumptions that may have informed your point of view. Our initial meeting to explain our feelings and concerns will take about two hours if we are both willing to engage and invest in the relationship. Egregious injuries may take as much as four hours initially. End of these meetings with a list of activities that each party will act upon. The hurt individual must propose something that can be done to ease the immediate shock and encourage the ongoing dialogue. Submission to this request is the apology that will suffice.

Principle-Motivated Action

You are guilty, and that motivates action. Make sure the action is informed, mindful, principle-motivated, corrective activity. Just like Mills demonstrated in his study, you feel guilty because you cheated and received a small prize. But, the choice is bigger than cheating, and the prize is beyond the tangible reward of that moment. The choice is relationship. The reward is learning. The question is sustainability. Focus on the sustainable choice to make at this moment.

You have to be informed. If you have hurt me, you have to get the information from me. Comprehend what I am hurt by, and what I propose as a remedy.

Be mindful of your own defensiveness and the origins of your decision to transgress. Little in the human mind is done by accident. Search your own feelings and intentions to determine if this action expresses some subconscious conflict. Just because you are capable of hiding it explicitly, does not prove the absence of the intention implicitly.

Identify the relationships, knowledge, roles, and environments that you value. Consider the behaviors and thoughts that would support those values. Articulate principles that undergird those values. Detail the immutable truths that are not subject to circumstance or peer pressure. If you are to honor those values, you must consider the people with whom you engage. You must consider the sources and methods you use to get information. You must define a role for yourself and understand the role you play in your social groups. Consider each of these in various contexts. If they are principle-motivated, the outcomes, the impact on those around you, and the products produced will be consistent with your intentions.

The Legacy Obligation

You can't go back. The focus is not just doing or succeeding. The focus is the process and recognition of the process. You must understand that you honor the previous generation by building upon the foundation provided (whatever that is). Your obligation to the last generation is to build. The obligation to the next generation is to provide information on the mechanism and insight about the mindset to persevere, enjoy, and connect with networks in a way that continues health and wealth creation.

SECTION III: DISILLUSIONMENT

Disillusionment: A motivation to accept appearances as collective delusion, hard work as a progressive outcome, and success as a destination.

CHAPTER 9
DISILLUSIONMENT: BARRIERS TO SUSTAINABILITY

And the Lord God said, "Who told you that you were naked?"
(Genesis 3:11)

Disillusionment describes your inability to articulate the process of the system and to see that your choices impact the current system and other systems. Stated another way, when you are disillusioned, you lack self-efficacy, and you lack system-awareness.

Addressing Disillusionment

To address your disillusionment, you will have to learn to construct the system with your choices as the basis for design. This is instead of relying on the system to provide you with trustworthy foundations. You will need to create habits that support mental health, evidence awareness of your impact, and illuminate the system overall. You will have to create objective ways to evaluate your progress—both learning and self-development. You will also need to evaluate your progress periodically, and correct any deficiencies.

System construction, productivity, relationship-building, and reflection are the basic abilities for staving off disillusionment. You have been taught to sabotage these productive abilities through an insistence on arrogance masquerading and values without principles.

Arrogance Masquerading

Why I'm Against Politeness

Politeness is not authenticity. As much as the two SHOULD be able to co-exist, politeness has the tendency to glaze over honest and consonant reflections of your judgments, motives, and capacity. The trouble is, to be truly polite, you have to be authentic. You have to be honest and forthcoming with your deficits, your desires, your ability, and your intentions. You have to be open to improvements in all these as a function of interaction with another person. That's true politeness. It is to be open to the influence of the other in a cultural sense.

As an educator, I am constantly made aware of this disconnect. I often see resistance to learning–a refusal to be uncertain while denying the process and tools I offer as professor. Many reasons exist for this, and I expect this phenomenon. What floors me every time is the "politeness" that greets my challenge of this inertia. "That's not politeness," I want to scream. "That's arrogance...unsustainable arrogance!"

My job as the best educator ever, is to move you from unsustainable arrogance to sustainable confidence. I need three things in order to accomplish this. First, I need your self-determination that you are willing to move as I inform your decision making. If not, know that this is willful ignorance–you just refused to move with a person you have hired to inform you choices. Second, I need you to own your deficits. If not, know that this is dishonesty–you are content to pretend rather than work toward being. Third, I need you to share authentically what you want within the context of your worldview. If not, know that this is unhealthy pride–you hold your SELF outside the scrutiny of others in order to maintain your self-protection and conceit.

The tendency of false politeness is to speak pleasantly while insisting on some combination of the following:

- **Refuse to learn.** You forcibly resist new information as irrelevant and useless. You feel that the new information threatens your world view when it often provides richness.
- **Cover your flaws.** You are not sure of your goal, destination, or motivation, but that should be beside the point in your mind. Uncertainty is the basis of our interaction. It is the basis of learning. If you were certain, there would be no need for learning.
- **Obscure what it is you really want.** Your desire may be looked upon as selfish or otherwise bad, so you keep it hidden. You don't realize that desire is only the inclination. Any desire can be sublimated into sustainable choices.
- **Deflect from your deficits in capacity.** Blame the other for something she is not doing. Rather than evaluating your contribution, you spend energy pointing out what the other is not doing.
- **Refuse to establish congruence between what you say and what you mean.** Say it in jest. Mumble it under your breath. Have the conversation with someone other than me, the person engaged in the learning transaction. Or, you express it in anger or frustration rather than committing to a

conversation. Here you call someone to a higher standard, but you do not engage in an opportunity for mutual growth, only an insistence on what you want to gain.

This all extends from an unfulfilled sense of self. You may not think of yourself as worthless, but you do think you are somewhat unworthy. You have not accepted and experienced the fact that you are enough. Most would think that the unsustainable arrogance extends from confidence, but it does not. Unsustainable arrogance is the result of a fear that if you give credence to new information, you may not be able to master it. You would then risk being judged as an amateur, a newbie, or a beginner. You would lose your place of privilege, and be relegated to the position of learner dependent upon a teacher.

A fulfilled sense of self would breed confidence. Not just a sense of yourself as worthy, but an allowance for new questions with the assurance that new information does not diminish your value. Genuinely accepting the role of learner and the dependence on a teacher is not failure or shameful. You still have the power to multiply your sources of knowledge, and you may apply your intellect to learn more quickly than any rational expectation.

A fulfilled sense of self is more than just the understanding of what you know and like to do. It also has the curiosity, sophistication, and capacity to explore and translate uncertain concepts to create relationships between new knowledge and what you already know and like to do. This translation is possible because you are confident in your goals AND committed to the process of achieving those goals. You may not know the how. In fact, it is more expedient that you not focus on the how. But, you know who YOU are. You are honest with your judgments, motives, and capacity even if they are unpopular and highlight your deficits, desires, ability, and intentions. You know that this authenticity allows you to seek and receive help to achieve the next step. You are open to allow me to share in your goals and process even if you have to admit that you did not achieve alone. Or, at least you are willing to allow me the chance to prove my worth as a guide along your journey.

True Confidence and Intelligence

Cognitive flexibility, the ability to move with ease from one attractor to another, is a hallmark of optimal intelligences. It is not vacillation between two ideas, but the ability to critically examine an idea on its merits EVEN if it is contrary to another strongly held idea. This is a seminal requirement of learning.

What I see among many instead is the tendency to argue vehemently outside the merits of the idea. They seem to stick to the argument as to a life raft on angry seas. They dare not venture into the water or the comparative improvement of a solid wooden boat for fear of losing the certainty of what they now float in.

Walking away disappointed, disposing of the relationship, refusing the conversation, fearing the argument, never risking being wrong is never committing to grow. You may make some mistakes, but your mistakes do not define you. When you give up saying, "I must be a mistake. I must be stupid," you communicate that you misunderstand the central pursuit. Learning is a danger without self-development. Seek both. You are not any of those derogatory adjectives. You are enough, and you are learning. Expanding your curiosity, sophistication, and capacity, you are also developing.

Instead of giving up, stay and discuss seeking to learn about the question at hand. Know that you may be ignorant of some facts, practiced in some unsustainable behaviors, and focused on insufficient goals. But, you are worthy of greater. Be willing to risk the embarrassment of growth. Be willing to put in the work based on our interaction--a certain guide--though you may be uncertain about the process.

The Power of Principles

You often exercise the fallacy of the characters in the ancient story. You seek to fulfill your role without articulating the undergirding principles. Your fallacy is to search for knowledge without an awareness of the opportunity for community, sensitivity to others, and clear indicators of success. Principled knowledge always produces self-development and growth for you and the community. In contrast, unprincipled achievement often selectively applies knowledge in order to maintain power of the few over the many.

Values without Principles. Your challenge is the same as that of any generation. You must rise to the stature of the previous generation, and continue a legacy of progress. A large amount of responsibility rests with each generation to provide roles and critical insight into the way things work. This combination of roles and insight are best encapsulated in principles that enable you, the next generation, to develop and apply values in the context of your environment. Principles remain unchanged, but the expression of the roles and application of insight changes to fit the issues, environments, and concerns of the day.

Many people describe ethics, morals, values, and principles synonymously. This conflation of words is a problem because it allows no word choice for your variability as an individual (values), your values influenced by your belief system and worldview (morals), your principles implemented as behaviors (ethics), and your closely-held, core constructs that are foundational to all the above (principles). The conflation leaves you unable to defend against your own sense of dissonance. You see yourself as conflicted and hypocritical without the vocabulary to articulate any differentiation. Let us differentiate principles as a specific concept.

The hierarchy of the principles lexicon is as follows from the most foundational and immutable to the most situational and variable: principles, ethics, morals, and values.

Values are your feelings or preferences. They vary according to the individual. **Morals** are values influenced by your belief system and worldview. They are the behaviors derived from rules applied to you. They describe what acceptable behavior is for you. **Ethics** are the behavioral application of principles. They are often codified in documents or purported as the basis of policy or rules. **Principles** are truths that are predictable regardless of situation or individual belief. They are closely-held, core constructs that are foundational to your judgments about behavior.

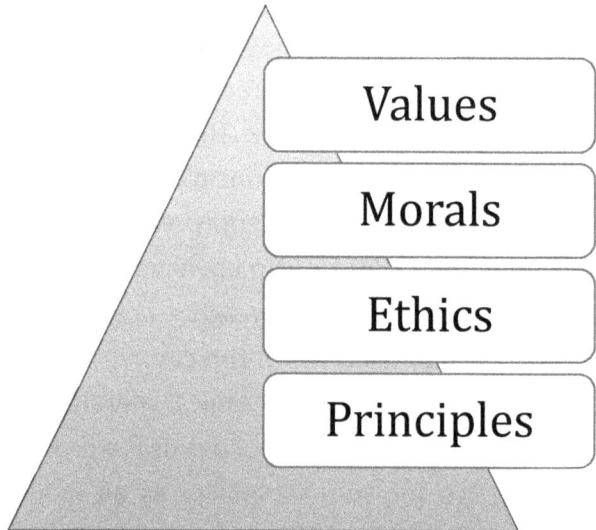

Values

Morals

Ethics

Principles

This differentiation is important because of the question of truth. Not "What is truth?" That question is immaterial. But, "What is the basis of the determination of truth?" Many base their judgements and therefore their decision making on values. That is, Values = Truth. Their arguments and justifications do not hold water because they are situation and belief bound. They adhere vehemently to the positions and preferences handed to them by the previous generation. Yet, they ignore or selectively identify with the issues, environments, and concerns of the day. The only way to maintain their positions is to limit their interaction or shame the other, contrary position through moral disengagement.

When the argument of the Values = Truth does not hold up, they use what Bandura calls **moral disengagement** tools to combat, ignore, or silence other points of view. You are probably familiar with the tools of moral disengagement. They are ego defenses and logical fallacies similar to our discussion of counterfeits in an earlier chapter. It should be noted that the use of moral disengagement can be correlated with decreased cognitive flexibility, lower creativity, and diminished empathy.

Most adopt moral disengagement in an attempt to maintain the honor of the previous generation. You often adopt it out of obligation to the generation before you. System construction, productivity, relationship-building, and reflection are limited to people and information that agree with your point of view. Others are called names and silenced through shaming. Without empathy for even the untoward position and an evaluation of principled choice behavior in action, you are lost—disillusioned.

Another option is Principle = Truth. In this equation, predictability and reasoned evaluation of the outcome and process form the basis of the argument. This equation also honors the information passed down from the previous generation, but it recognizes the principle communicated and translates it for the issues, environments, and concerns of the current day. Principle = Truth is characterized by cognitive flexibility, creativity, and empathy. It engages in conversations agreeing to disagree on values while seeking evidence, indications of validity, and the repeatable outcomes of reliability as the foundation for new questions. Not the confirmation of what is truth, but the motivation for continued questioning.

CHAPTER 10
MOVING PAST REDRESS IN THE GENERATIONAL NARRATIVE

Disillusionment Case Study: 1 of 3

Our story read from the ancient text continues with our main characters Adam and Eve. They have just been found in the garden the creator had prepared for them. The creator called to Adam, and Adam hid. Adam explained that he was afraid because he was naked. Adam went on to point out god's mistake in giving him Eve to beguile him.

We rejoin the story as the creator speaks what may be seen as punishment to Adam and Eve. To the woman the creator said, "You will bear children with pain. You will desire your husband." To the man, the creator said, "You will work the land with sweat. That is how you will eat. And, eventually you will die."

The creator, as the story continues, made garments of skin for the man and the women. He removed Adam and Eve from the garden. He made them cultivators. The woman's cultivation was centered in relationship and emotional attachment. The man's cultivation was centered in the satisfaction of achievement and the certainty of legacy. Their desire for knowledge was met with a new skilled endeavor. Their tendency toward consumerism was met with training in production. Both were pointed toward a truth that each choice has consequence for YOU and for US. Rather than see their fate as punishment, consider that this pronouncement is a pattern for principle creation tailored specifically to your needs.

And such is the situation for you in regard to your parents. You have been similarly put "out of the garden" into the unsure world of adulthood. At first blush, it seems that you have been abandoned. Some parents and children struggle to undo this natural maturity with disastrous results for the community at large. But, that resistance is born out of a feeling that separation of the child from the parent is a negative experience. It is necessary. It is the establishment of a new relationship. No longer parent to child. Now, adult to adult. It is a relationship characterized no longer by rules and simple values. Now, the principles must be understood and applied to new environments. For parents reading this, know that your task is to communicate beyond the values and the behaviors. You must engage the discussions and indicators of ethics and principle, allowing the child to exhibit his or her decision making ability. For the ill-prepared adult reading this, it is time to identify the principles that will outline your options, structure your decision making, and measure your adult contribution to our community.

In order to move beyond simple values, you will need to identify **new roles** outlining your daily activity and knowledge expansion. You will require **clear boundaries** that engage your curiosity, inform your role, and result in products. You must develop a respect for relationship, intimacy, and legacy as **indicators** of enduring success. No matter the characteristics of your history with your parents, you reach adulthood with an inclination, a signature energy, and a choice architecture reinforcing sustainable or unsustainable choices. This is the task of redress, to come to terms with the generational narrative you have been given.

Roles versus Obligation or Vengeance

A great experience with your parents tends toward a sense of obligation for you as an adult. A wanting experience with your parents tends toward vengeance or a need to correct the mistakes of your parents. Both are extremes that are unsustainable. Your task in adulthood is not a response to the previous generation. It is the establishment of your contribution. The focus is more sustainably placed on establishing a clear identity and your role in the world. You then outline your goals, daily choice architecture, and knowledge sources.

Your inclination is, if you are honest, to make your parents care, or to make them proud. Knowing that you want your parents to care enables a role decision. You can choose to be a slave to the expectations of your parents, or you can choose to find your purpose within your interests and giftedness.

You must figure and be consonant with what you care about. You must determine what actions you will perform in order to demonstrate that caring. Planning within your context, informed by multiple and competing sources can sustain gains as you define your new role. Seek authenticity and legacy. You owe the generations that come after you. That's how you honor the generations that came before you.

Capability versus Emulate or Repudiate

Affirming experiences with your parents support emulation— a desire to be like them, to do what they did. Negative experiences with your parents support repudiation—a strong inclination to do anything other than what your parents did. But, neither of these is YOUR option for your generation. Your options center on opportunity to determine and build your capability. Engage your curiosity. Construct products. Learn about markets. You measure success by how keenly you recognize and manipulate the process. The mechanisms and insights of capability inform the mindset to persevere, the enjoyment of your giftedness, and the connection with networks in a way that supports wealth creation.

Developing the mindset to persevere, you focus your energy on those things that you do well. Consider how you will sustain that ability incorporating new abilities, accessing new markets, expanding your impact. Enjoyment of giftedness is the mechanism through which your activity pays forward the opportunity—not the opportunity afforded by the previous generation, but the opportunity of the ability to choose in this moment. You have the chance. Now, give someone else that chance. Connect with networks to create legacy by sharing your giftedness with others. You create new disciples to the philosophy of capability and production. You spread a message of the possible. Finding the fit is the key to their success. Your fearless expression of your gift offers them the chance to find theirs.

Learning versus Superiority or Shame

Great experiences with parents lend themselves to feelings of superiority and status. Poor experiences with parents lend themselves to feelings of shame and waywardness. But, those are reactions to parenting. Your adult task beyond the generational narrative is to continue the learning in your generation through a respect for relationship, intimacy, and legacy as indicators of enduring success.

Just like Adam in the ancient story, your inclination is to hide your dysfunction. With great experiences with parents, it is the fear that you will never live up to their example. In response to poor experiences with parents, it is the fear that you have not learned the lessons needed to excel. In hiding your flaws, you attempt to reconstitute your parents into what you desire them to be for your comfort. You meditate on the life that you want so desperately beginning with your role in your family.

But, as an adult, your impact extends beyond your family of origin. Release yourself from any associated status or uncertainty related to your parent's worldview and their view of your options. Evaluate yourself holistically. Assess whether you are sustainably suited for your goals. Launch from the nest of your parents. Develop your unique and active definition of your impact on the world. The value of that impact points forward to your children's children, not backward to your parents.

Honest is Better than Right: Seeking the Non-Dual Existence

The challenge is to live your life, not the life that was structured or predicted by your parents. Realize that they introduced and reinforced views, but you determine the narrative from today forward. It's not just about determining wrong. Existence is greater than the dichotomy of right and wrong.

Change Theories. Whether Transtheoretical model, Roger's change model, Generalist Intervention Model, they all begin with the expectation of denial. What if your imperative was not to change, but to integrate what you have and develop it into its most sustainable form?

Human choice behavior cannot be reduced to simple black, white, and gray. The first step is to let go of the duality of rights and wrongs, good and evil, good or bad. Human choice behavior has **color**. Simply stated: your goals, tolerance, and will determine your choice behavior. More specifically: choice is a function of will through a sense of self-efficacy, influenced by consciousness in the context of institutions representing an enduring mindset.

You determine whether your choices are sustainable or unsustainable based on the expectation of outcome. Decision making weighs both negative and positive outcomes and their impact both short and long-term. Both states are present at the same time. Your goal, even subconsciously, is to maintain balance. Discernment is needed in order to make the choice behavior practical and progressive.

Human choice behavior has color. The true nature of discernment is to determine the energy resonance. Defined based on the physics, energy resonance is the reinforcement or extending of personal energy by reflection or in-tune vibration of another person. Consider that the requirement within energy resonance is true or valid frequency—what we would call honesty or authenticity. It is not a requirement to be clear and consistent in vibration. It is a requirement to say what you mean, reflect you true intentions, and be the person your behavior says you are.

Let go of the need to CHANGE and the limitations of DUALITY. Let go of the insistence on being RIGHT. Replace these with the energy of INTEGRATION, NON-DUAL (Both-And), and HONESTY.

Your Energy After Disappointment

You have power. Even when you are treated unfairly, overworked with underpay, or cheated on. How are you using it?

Blame and Rationalization. These are people who spend time seemingly attempting to gain others to their point of view. Their main complaint is that they have been wronged. It is important to speak up, to seek answers, and to seek justice at every level. That's not what you are doing when you focus on blame and rationalization. The decision has been made. It was not fair. You have explored recourse. None exists. At this point, any energy spent is energy against a brick wall. There is another way.

Responsibility and Investment. It is time to seek another route to your destination. It could be that the investments you were making were misplaced. But, first and foremost, you must realize that the outcomes are up to you. Take YOUR POWER back. Take ownership of your energy. You arrest that power by taking responsibility for the choices you make and the energy you attract. Spend your time confirming your energy and seeking resonance from other sources. Find the space and relationships that are compatible with your vibrations.

Waiting on Karma. When you watch for natural laws to manifest, you upset elements of order and may be misapplying your energy reserves. Karma is one such natural law. Your hopeful watch on the lookout for karma expends energy you could apply as attraction for your next small success. See these as real investments. Make the most sustainable investment possible. Rather than waste your vision on the manifestation of karma, trust blindly that karma will fulfill its purpose. Your task is to fulfill your purpose.

When Your Energy is Off

Stress is energy. Happiness is energy. The key understanding is that you attract the events that connect with the energy you wallow in and you exude. When the stress increases, do you curse and despair, or do you plan and execute? The situation changes based on how you react. Your energy is like the call of birds. Specific calls attract specific birds. The skill required is to manage your energy and your vibrations intentionally—to intentionally attract what is compatible.

Attracting the Best

Life has curves and challenges. But, I'm offering the insight that the next struggle is opportunity, not just because of your cognitive reframe, but because YOU attract the best with your attitude, your vocalizations, your patterns of resolve, and your choices. As my current favorite quote states, "The universe is rigged in your favor." Vibrate with faith, self-efficacy, and consciousness. Enjoy the results.

Following is the foundation strategy:

1. Identify the goals, desires, impact, and mindset you want to have and influence others to have. Write it down, and post it until you memorize it.

2. Open up to who you are complete with your quirks, pet peeves, hurts, needs, and giftedness. Integrate these realities through sustainable rules that support choice behavior that gets you to your goals.

3. Seek understanding and insight to see the choices of others as reasonable. Let go of the need to judge blame until after you understand motive and mechanism.

4. Accept that your incompatibility with some people and environments is based on the energy within those environments. Maintain the honesty of your vibrations through "sound checks" in your private, trusted, safe places and relationships. Seek compatible energy resonance to improve your quality of life.

Curiosity, Consumerism, and Consequences

Beyond the constraints of duality, the choices are not as finite as stay or leave. In a non-dual existence, you *can* beyond limits. Can what? Emphasize the CAN without worrying about the WHAT. This means that you are complete even before the choices are made. This truth makes all options available to you. Any limiting is not truth. It is an intrusion from outside of you seeking to control for some purpose outside of you.

In our story from the ancient text, Adam and Eve condemned themselves to a dualistic existence. In this view, they were stuck with the choice to evaluate their behavior as right or wrong. But, the hope was that, through exploration of the consequences, they would realize both what they were losing and the awareness that they could have had it all. That is, that right and wrong provides an elementary and incomplete option set.

Curiosity

Adam and Eve desired knowledge. They were **curious** about what they did not know. For the male, it was an attempt to find answers about origin and purpose. For the female, it was an attempt to test connections and reveal intimacy. The consequence tasked them with a new skilled endeavor requiring a new perspective. The quest for purpose now met problem solving, research & archival, generational learning, and the mote of wisdom. The quest for intimacy now met nurture, attachment, reciprocity, and relationship.

Non-dual existence understands that learning and application include purpose. Curiosity is what motivates us to grow beyond our current boundaries. The result is both a loss of the familiar and a freedom to explore within the unknown. As it was for Adam and Eve, your curiosity must grow to understand that skills are the expression of principles, which motivate sustainable choice behavior. Identify the principles that correspond with your desires.

Consumerism

Adam and Eve tended toward consumerism. They wanted to **utilize** their uniqueness and privilege as sentient beings who themselves held the power to create. For the male, it was an attempt to create from his own hands. For the female, it was a hope to capture the miracle for herself. The consequence exposed them to training in production. The quest of the hands met the process of planting, watering, defending, pruning, harvesting, and storing. The quest for miracle met conception, carrying, preparing, birthing, and swaddling.

Both, from a dualistic view, end in the loss of the creation. Non-dual reality reveals that the mechanism of perpetual energy creation is the reciprocity of production and consumption in balance. Loss occurs only when the reciprocity and balance relationship are lost. Similar to Adam and Eve, your consumption must grow to understand the reciprocal cycle of creation, use, and renewal necessary for balance. This means that you produce in order to disseminate. You raise up relationships in order to launch them into new relationships. The cycle continues, sunrise and sunset.

Consequences

Both Adam and Eve learned what we must learn. It is truth that each choice has **consequence**. Each action has a reaction. As much as this is expression of universal law, it is also expression of our sense of purpose and order extending from our individual identities. The male sought control in the opportunity to be. The female sought stability in the opportunity to persist. The search for existence was met with a rule of reciprocity: you reap what you sow. Assurance of opportunity is a result of doing your honest part. The search for stability was met with another rule of endurance: love suffers all. Assurance of reward is the result of consistency and patience.

Dualistic views see consequences as either beneficial or punitive. Non-dual reality realizes that consequences are always beneficial as a matter of perspective and opportunity. Awareness and respect for the natural laws of balance, attraction, reciprocity, and energy conservation, beyond simple adherence to rules, is the beginning of wisdom. Like Adam and Eve, understand that consequences undergird destiny, expectations, and predictions extending from options. Change and consequences are all that is certain. You control both through the function of your individual, adult identity.

CHAPTER 11
BEYOND THE GENERATIONAL NARRATIVE

Disillusionment Case Study: 2 of 3

Returning to our story from the ancient text, Adam and Eve have now learned of the consequences of their fall. For Adam, he was to toil in labor attempting to cultivate food from the ground. For Eve, she was to toil in childbirth with a longing for her husband. But, more was revealed.

The Creator realized that access to the tree of life would result in the couple living forever. The creator discussed the problem. "He has now become like one of us." To remedy this contradiction, and cement the consequence, the creator banished the couple from the garden. They were removed from their familiar surroundings. They were disconnected from constant access to the source of creation. They were successfully launched into autonomous existence to continue the exercise of free will.

Their disobedience carried consequences. Adam and Eve were tempted to dwell on the consequences as a punishment that left them outside the protection of the garden. But, the true loss was a loss of communication, even communion with the creator. They were now challenged to make their own way without the daily visit from their creator.

But even in this, all is not lost. The interaction was not LOST. It needed to be engaged in differently. It is just the same with you and your launch into adulthood. It seems that you have been cut off from the innocence and plausible deniability of youth. That is true. You have. But, you also have the opportunity to engage in the world differently than you have before. Your status as an adult means that your relationships are not as they were before. They will never return to the prior relationship. You have to establish a new relationship, a new way of interacting.

The context of this integration is most analogous to the establishment of adult relationships with your parents. The parent-child relationship is a suitable beginning for the discussion. It brings in elements of longing, growth, and maturity. You will need to learn to distinguish between healthy and unhealthy relationships. Not every adult is as great as your supportive parent. Not every adult is as absent as your worst parent. You must understand that adulthood is founded on your experiences of being parented, yet also have little to do with reconciling those experiences. They stand alone sustainable or unsustainable. I propose three important functions to discern as you mature beyond the generational narrative you were given, and as you begin to script your own narrative to the next generation. Discern the potential for collaboration, engage mentors and platonic partnerships, and distinguish romantic relationships. These are the skills underlying the competency of **establishing adult relationships**. You will need to commit to developing these skills, continually gaining competence.

The Potential for Collaboration

Satisfaction & Reason

Seriously, soberly identify what you need. When it comes to your needs, the insight lies beyond the want. You must understand the mechanism. How many times have you decided that you want a pizza slice or a hamburger based on clever visual advertising ploy? The mechanism included lighting, camera angles, specific selection, and inclusion of some elements that may not even be edible. These visual cues connect to your memory and emotion tied to the burger. You translate this as a craving for the item. Your hunger, if present, can be satisfied with a number of options. But, the mechanism, because it connects with your memory and emotion, steers you toward the hamburger as a specific satisfier. Your "want" of the hamburger could also be stated as you "remember" the hamburger. In this example, the mechanism makes the connection between want and memory with or without the "need" of hunger present.

Serious, sober evaluation of your options attempts to connect the emotional response with logic for a complete analysis of the context of choice and the potential outcomes of each option is chosen. This is understanding the mechanism—awareness of the options accounting for emotion, reason, context, and consequence. You may ask questions similar to the following:

1. What are my felt needs?
2. Why do I feel they will satisfy?
3. What is the mechanism involved?
4. What are the side effects of this choice?
5. What other options might I select that accomplish the same satisfaction without the side effects?

For example, Coffee works in the morning. Alcohol works after a stressful day. The Why of Coffee: caffeine is a stimulant. You value the pick-me-up of the stimulant in the morning. You may also have connected memory through the smell of fresh coffee grounds and the emotion of shared cups with a loved one. The Why of Alcohol: alcohol is a depressant. You value the relaxing effect of the depressant. You may have connected memory through the thought of sophisticated and attractive people who drink your brand of alcohol. You may have connected the emotion of fun had while drinking or the feeling of openness or perceived relaxation.

My point is a requirement that you realize the mechanism in the context of your felt need. You can get the same stimulation in the morning through exercise. Your blood will flow. Your breathing will quicken. You will be energized for the day. You can get the same relaxation through meditation. Your blood pressure will settle. Your breathing will be more intentional. You will calm and relax. With both these new options, the challenge is not in reaching the same goal. It is in addressing your memory and emotion tied to the options, especially if you have more experience with one option over another. The challenge to replace coffee and alcohol with exercise and meditation is centered in memory and emotion—a visceral connection that leaves out the consideration of reason, context, and consequence.

I begin with this example as a foundation for discernment of relationships. Establishing healthy adult relationships is not a simple matter of want based on memory and emotion. It also includes a reasonable evaluation of sustainability based on your desired outcomes. It reviews the context of the opportunity and other options that are available. It predicts the consequence of each choice and compares those outcomes against your desired outcomes. Whether the determination is for a business partner, a mentor, or a romantic partner, the process of examination is the same. Each of these are collaborators.

Especially when betrayal strikes, you are tempted to experience your emotional world as simple dichotomous choices like to trust or not to trust. But, adult emotion management is much more complex than this simple choice. Emotional maturity includes the ability to recognize the capacity of the other in relationships and the ability to tailor your expectations to fit the reality in the relationship. In other words, you ask the question of whether to trust, to trust with how much, what situations impact capacity, and how to prepare for the results you expect. In adult relationships, you will find that your labeling of relationships extends beyond the simple dichotomy of "friend" or "enemy" to describe many levels of engagement.

Capacity of the Person

Understand emotional capacity as similar to weight capacity. Consider a person that has no trouble carrying 25 lb dumbbells. If you increase the weight to 50 lb dumbbells, this new weight will impact his/her ability to function. He/she may not be able to carry the weight.

In this same way, there are people in your life that have the capacity to manage their emotional state and function admirably. But, these same admirable persons would fail if tasked with considering your feelings, bearing your burdens, or collaborating alongside you. The increased emotional complexity that is consideration of your emotions adds weight that they have trouble balancing. No matter the "supposed" capability or the position they hold in your life or an organization, they just cannot carry the additional weight. Your insistence, clarification of your load, or other entreats will not increase their capacity. Seek others in your life who have the capacity to handle themselves, consider your feelings, and vision for your work in partnership.

Fitting Your Expectations to Their Capacity

Wall up or Wall down are not the only emotional options. Your challenge is to build gradually in mutual emotional support. Rather than all or nothing tests of loyalty, consider engaging with others on a schedule of increasing emotional sharing. When you discern that you have reached the limit of the other's capacity for emotional support, note that capacity. Rather than disowning the person because of their capacity level, endeavor to engage them only up to their emotional capacity. You do not have to sever associations because they are not the best of supportive friends.

Keep in mind that emotional capacity describes a person's ability to engage with you in mutually sustainable, emotionally healthy ways. Do not get into the habit of expecting just because someone is "family" or knows you for a long time or "should be" emotionally empowering to you.

Adult realization includes the knowledge that it is your responsibility to manage your energy and empowerment through careful selection of sustainable interactions. The relationships you were born into can be maintained, but you must also see them for what they are rather than what you wish they were.

Shades of Emotional Engagement

Consider that between friend and enemy, many levels of engagement exist. These levels are tied to the capacity of the other and your expectations for engagement.

Level	Engagement-Capacity
Confidant/ Protagonist	Intentional feeding of your energy and emotional management reserves. Engagement can be viewed as sacrificial—engaging you to the seeming detriment of the other. Capacity is beyond what you are able to measure.
Friend	Awareness of your needs is increased. Effort is made to emotionally empower. Capacity is limited only by ability, but never by desire or intention.
Associate/Helper	Task-based engagement. Little consideration of your specific needs, but general accommodation is made. Capacity is limited to certain environments and to assist toward specific goals.
Neighbor/Peer/Co-Worker	Neutral impact on energy. Unexplored engagement other than cordiality. Unexplored capacity.
Competitor/ Rival/Nemesis	Expend energy toward your goals but in opposition to the other. Engagement is adversarial. Capacity is limited to support of the oppositional interaction.
Enemy	Causes energy drain with little movement toward goals often frustrating goals. Engagement is only in conflict. Capacity is adverse and seeks to disrupt emotional management.
Archenemy/ Antagonist	Intentional drain on your energy. Engagement is deceitful and mis-representative. Capacity is toward dis-empowerment in order to leave you broken.

Multiple Mentors & Platonic Partners

A New Role for Parents. Your parents may have been one source of help and support. Whether they were or not, your status as an adult requires a new approach and an evolution of your relationships with your parents and with others. You are no longer under the protection of parents. You are now in the role of protégé. The relationship is no longer directive. It must now become instructive.

Protégé communicates the right amount of balance realized in the guide and influence of parents. For good or for ill, the people that you looked to in your formative years impact the foundations, calculations, thresholds, and capacity you utilize to make your choices. You do yourself a disservice to attempt denial. It is more sustainable to recognize your current state, and seek to inform your growth and development. The best of parental models only provide what they can with the expectation that you will add more. The worst of parental models demonstrate what you want to avoid. The common thread between the two is choice. You always have a choice.

Now instructive, your relationship with your parents is predicated upon your choice. You are no longer required to live within their set of rules. You have access to information beyond their control. Their words, patterns, and temperament linger while you grow to develop your own. But, it is important to realize how much your growth is seeded in soil cultivated by your parents. This realization can be the foundation of the search for new soil—a new mental and emotional starting point for your choice behavior. You are free to choose integration of your parents in a new role or diminishing of their role for whatever reason. Of course, they are always "your parents," but the impact of that phrase on your choices MUST change as you sustainably engage your adult roles and responsibility.

Mentors

Imagine if you had someone who thinks you are special and gifted. Someone who thinks about your success constantly. Someone who knows the systems you will encounter. Someone who will work with you to develop the tools to reach the levels you want to reach in your profession and in life. Someone who focuses on the perfection of your honesty rather than your faults. Someone who requires only that you succeed as payment for this investment.

I know that you may not have a defined space for a person like this. I know you may be fearful of such a relationship. From your perspective, this may sound too good to be true. Your decision whether to trust is not made easier because this person is packaged in human form and standing before you.

All I can offer is the definition and a name for this person. This person is called a mentor, and I am the best. The choice now rests with you. You may only see two options. You see your Option 1 to con me only seeking to get what you want. You see your Option 2 to respectfully disengage from any relationship and limit our interaction. But, more options exist. Do yourself a favor, and attend to the following:

1. **Rethink Mentoring.** Multiple supports are best to address the variety of contexts, institutions, and knowledge areas that you will need to face during your lifetime.

2. **Match Needs and Supports**. Certain of a clear understanding of needs including mechanisms, you must connect potential supports to needs, create intentional pathways for targeted support, and maintain systematic review of support performance.

3. **Risk to Complete Your Mentor List.** It is not natural for everyone to connect with mentors and supports. It can be, but it is not always.

Risk may be the hardest. I am asking you to trust. But, I am NOT asking you for blind trust. You must develop and apply the skills to Risk, Discern, and Learn. The common decision of whether to struggle alone attempting to prove yourself or to engage vulnerably seeking help fits into these three categories.

Risk. You may not feel comfortable risking even in a supportive relationship. Fear of rejection keeps some from reaching out. This is solved through a clear understanding of the contribution the mentor makes to your development. It may be as time-limited as a 15-minute session. It could even be as simple as a late response to a text message. They don't have to be a confidant or therapist, ready for hour-long sessions. The mentor only need be a listening ear, a ready resource broker, or an informed answer to questions.

Of course, it is a risk to trust someone. Any partnership is risky. But, ask yourself what you have to give up in order to participate in this partnership. Are you able to maintain appropriate boundaries? What is the structure of the transaction—meaning what does this potential partner want in return? Risk is a fact of life. Sustainable risk is the key to immense rewards.

Discern. You may have trouble making the connection in a meaningful way. Ask questions. Don't ask for commitments. Realize that you, as the requestor, are the one who must put forth the effort to maintain the interaction. You are the beneficiary of the time investment. Advanced relationships, a hallmark of the best mentors, are marked by a request for reciprocity. It may be collaborative research, a conference presentation, or a co-author opportunity, but these mentors are skilled in developing the relationship based on the development of a mutually beneficial project.

A fact packaged along with risk is that people will let you down. Judge whether the mentor has a reputation for betrayal, malfeasance, or impropriety. Then, judge the results of the relationship. Is the mentor supporting you to be better? Is your experience with the mentor informing your ability to mentor?

Trusting does not mean you give away your power to investigate and determine that you have outgrown a mentor. In fact, the best of mentors work toward your growth—the outgrowing of the mentor-mentee relationship toward a collegial relationship.

Learn. You may have trouble maintaining the connection without the feeling that you are bothering the mentor or overusing the support. The great thing about a mentor, a good one, is that they give you the truth with no chaser. That means, if you are bothering them, they will let you know. They will tell you how to get the help you need from someone else. Or, they will tell you to buck up and deal. Either way, you can trust the advice because you have benefitted from similar directly-presented advice in the past.

Learning to risk wisely, with eyes open, is difficult, but it is a lesson that continually pays dividends. Learning to judge the fruit produced from an individual and the fruit from a relationship is a lesson of leadership. The lesson: The difference between using someone and partnering with them is the reciprocity of the relationship. An interaction in which only one person gets what they want is a con. An interaction in which both persons gain is a team.

Platonic Partnership

The Potential for Business. Our relationship grows as we get to know each other better. Our opportunity grows as we outline new ventures and products. For example, when you find out that I want to produce a training video targeting females and self-worth, you may organize a forum and partner with me to film it. Over the years, this partnership can benefit us both.

I know others have abused this opportunity, and made the specter more fearful. But, again, make your own boundaries. You do not have to risk all. Realize what you are risking—time, emails, and the stigma of being helped. Contrary to the prevailing belief, no one succeeds alone.

The challenge is to choose partners that make you better, to connect with a team that causes you to achieve more than you thought possible. If that is not your experience even after one project, you have not lost anything you were not prepared to lose. But, if extraordinary is what you experience after one quarter of partnership, imagine the potential over many years.

Differences between Men & Women. Remember the case study from the ancient text. Men were handed the consequence of working the land through sweat and toil. Women were handed the consequence of desiring a mate. These consequences, and the inclinations they create, may cause challenges in partnerships that are not intended to be romantic. Without mental and emotional health, either party could be stuck in the longing for help to meet physical needs while the relationship is most sustainably maintained for progress toward another set of goals. Stated plainly, sex threatens to complicate and eventually destroy otherwise productive relationships. Hijacking of professional relationships by sexual engagement is always founded in mental and emotional need that is proposed to be addressed through physical intercourse. Fundamentally, it is the consequence of the needs of the male or the female manifesting as an insistence on "going back" rather than "moving forward." For the male, it is a need to demonstrate power, control, and authority of conquest. An immature expression of an inkling of what adulthood is about. For the female, it is a need to find nurture, support, and creativity in relationship. An incomplete cross-section of the time and investment required for healthy adult relationships.

The solution to this is the same as it was in separating from the parental obligation. Remember your B.E.S.T.—**B**oundaries, **E**quifinality, **S**tructure of Transactions, and **T**ransactions. Boundaries refer to the transparency of the relationship. Be honest with yourself about the presence of an attraction, your mental acuity, and your emotional states. This honest review enables the creation of rules of engagement and management of your needs. The lines are not blurred and certainly not crossed. Equifinality ensures that you harbor no illusion that "you are the only one"—a signature feature of narcissism. Both persons in the relationship should understand that this is not a "soul mate" interaction, however comfortable the interaction presents. Many other options and relationships may provide this same opportunity for progress and growth. Structure of Transactions necessitates a clear presentation of the process and expectations within the relationship. Both parties present what they want to receive. Both are open to giving in service to the relationship. Both parties understand what it takes to achieve success. Transaction is a consistent monitoring of the relationship according to progress goals. If progress is not being made, the relationship should be curtailed unless a new structure of transaction can be agreed upon. Distraction from progress precipitates the deception clouding the purpose of the relationship resulting in unsustainable choices and disillusionment once you realize that the relationship was not built to fulfil certain needs.

The Switch to Investing Sustainability in Romance

No Need to be Nice

I talked with a 20-something college student a while back. She told me about a guy—friend of a friend—who asked her for a date. She went on the date. She felt uncomfortable with the guy, and ended the date early. The guy proceeded to prophesy to her about how sad her life will be if she can't recognize a "nice" guy when she sees one. She left him sitting in his car mid-sentence. He yelled after her, "Call me when you calm down!"

She related this story to me a day after the encounter. I assured her that she was not wrong for following her feelings. I explained that his behavior after her decision to end the date was troubling. Knowing how this story has gone in the past for other girls, I suggested that she not allow loneliness or boredom to influence her into calling the guy again.

I talked with her a week later. She had called the guy! "What happened?"

"I was feeling bored, so I called," she admitted.

"So, was it the great cure for boredom you had hoped?" I asked.

"Not a chance," she said. "We just ended up arguing."

I was a bit heartbroken. At the same time, I had been proven right once again—a common occurrence due to my years practice and observation. It is boredom, loneliness, and unsustainable curiosity that supports unsustainable choices. These insecurities are a problem. AND, the problem is also the Jedi mind trick of polite society based in double-standards and sexist expectations of women. Some guys understand the trick's utility, and seek to trick women into going along with the conformity.

My Counsel to My Daughters

While reading the posts from other conversations between guys and girls, I formulated some thoughts. I want to make sure my daughters are not tricked. I was especially dismayed at the language and name calling my daughters may have to endure from self-styled "nice" guys. I hope to provide counsel that communicates to my daughters that the mind-games and guilt trips attempted by some guys are desperate attempts of insecurity to capitalize on perceived insecurities. The solution is the certainty of authenticity, self-respect, integrity, and a holistic sense of self.

Being Authentic is ALWAYS more sustainable than Being Nice

You do not owe anything to anyone. Make your choices intentionally. You can always change your mind, but never allow his bullying or anyone else's force into your decision making process. You don't owe any specific answer. You don't owe a conversation. You don't have to be polite or nice or cordial. Be you. Realize that your "mean" actions did not invite name calling. Your authentic, intentional, sustainable actions set the standard of your character and revealed his character.

A Compliment is never worth your Self-Respect

His or anyone's attempts at being "nice" are to be evaluated through YOUR filter. Realize that "trying to be nice" is not the goal. Your reaction doesn't determine the character of the other person. They were that person even prior to your interaction. You will be more fulfilled engaging with people who are authentic. You can see their intention more clearly when you are authentic. Seek authenticity rather than vain compliments. And, when compliments have an air of disrespect or inappropriateness, accept that this too is vanity. Many compliments will be trite and empty, but even compliments with more substance cannot be surrogates for true authenticity revealed in actions consistent with words.

YOU set Your Expectations of Your Behavior

An easy way to tell the character of a person is by listening to their expectations of you. It is NEVER appropriate for a suitor or would-be friend to make expectations of your behavior that violate your desired action. In other words, real friends support your choices. If they want you to fit into their expectations, they evidence insecurities that will continue to be a hindrance to your hope for sustainable relationship. Great relationships add to who you are, challenge you to reach higher, and support your success. But, even if you choose to go against the hopes of a real friend, they allow you your choice.

Trust your instincts in Romantic Relationships

If you have the feeling that you should leave, the action to take is to leave. If you have a vibe that a person is not healthy for you, the response is to distance yourself. Listen to your instincts. They are a natural way to discern through the words and the compliments and the expectations and your own wishes. If your encounter with a person making requests of you made you angry and stressed or uncomfortable, this is not a relationship to go back to after you are chill and calm. It is a relationship to be avoided. Politeness, "nice," does not apply here. As I have said, it NEVER applies. Neither does curiosity...or boredom...or loneliness. Not here.

Engage in relationships that are empowering. Be you without apology. Expect respect in each word and action. Hold your standard and expect a high standard. Trust your reason and emotion together. You will invite authenticity, respect, integrity, and holism.

CHAPTER 12
REWRITING YOUR STORY

Disillusionment Case Study: 3 of 3

In the final installment of our guiding case, the fall is complete. The consequences have been handed down and realized. One final detail remains to be unpacked. The Creator, presumably fearing that Adam and Eve would attempt to gain re-entry to the garden, placed an angel armed with a flaming sword to guard the way to the tree of life. A curious action if not for the analogy it makes possible.

Human nature believes that after punishment, "Someday we can go back to the way it was before." The preoccupation was with returning to the way things were—a system of simple roles and free-time. Now, no easy way to success exists. The phrases "pain of labor" and "by the sweat of your brow" emote a path of hard work and risk. But, if the risk is well founded, and the work is sustained, a reward can be obtained.

No. You can't go back physically. Just as Adam and Eve were barred by an angel with a flaming sword in our story, you are barred from physically returning to your youthful innocence and frivolity.

But, you can create a new foundation mentally and emotionally. You can learn the lessons of your youth, and practice a purity of thought. You can create beauty and coping behaviors. You can gain a perspective of emotion as energy realizing the sway you hold on what is attracted to you. You can realize your impact on the next generation through the energy you practice, what you attract, and the training you provide.

Your focus is best placed on building a foundation for the next generation. This is legacy. Refuse the example of Adam and Eve, who learned through further disappointment not managing the temperament and sense of collaboration among their two boys Cain and Abel.

You cannot go back. Your past is your past. Your experiences have shaped you. BUT! You can rewrite your narrative as a foundation for success. Your new narrative will not be an illusion that you must maintain, but it can be the self-fulfilling prophecy of success rather than failure. The power of the mind is to order the body toward a contemplated purpose. This means that the purpose you contemplate most often will be the purpose that your body is poised to achieve.

Posture of Purpose

A fist may be raised into the air before it moves to strike the table. Bodies are positioned at the edge of the chair before the legs are engaged to stand from a sitting position. Observers have a good idea of what a person will do based on his/her posture. Your posture must be one that causes those around you to expect your success. In addition to the physical reaction within you, those around you will support your success through their expectation that falls in line with your expectation.

Your posture is weighed down with trauma, fraud, fantasy, and victimization. These are feelings that you have about yourself that insidiously find their way into your definition of self. The feelings themselves have no place within your definition. The fact that you overcame or have the potential to overcome, is fodder for your definition of self.

Your challenge is to do what everyone has said, but no one has walked you through: to deal with it. What you have experienced will not just go away. You will not just "get over it." Trauma leaves scars. Feelings of not good enough cause you to second guess yourself. Fantasies about what could have been inhibit your focus. Victim mentality limits your action.

Beyond excuses, denial, and suppression, you can deal with your reality in a healthy way that organizes your past fears and enables your posture of purpose. The Shelving Process offers a way to engage, process, integrate, and overcome your experience.

Shelving Process

1. Mental Component: Build a mental shelf to organize your experiences. Place the experiences in notebooks to be placed on that shelf. In these notebooks, mentally record the issues, your experiences, and the lessons.

2. Physical Component: Physically write open and honest and free letters to the people, issues, and things that challenge your health and well-being. You can choose whether to burn, bury, or bequeath the letters.

3. Overcome misinformation and negative self-talk by writing your own narrative. Renew your reality with the opportunity to consider that you can learn from and adopt the healthy,

supported, and triumphant experiences of others as your backstory.

4.   Move from "parents" and "respected adults" to "colleagues" in your adult relationships. Establish your goals for each new relationship based on your role and expertise. The relationship and counsel of colleagues is valued according to the example of their lives and the impact of the relationship and followed counsel in your life.

Shelving Analogy: The Mental Component

Your experiences must become like project notebooks on a shelf. Dealing with them means first acknowledging that they are real. Understand that realization of your experiences is a process. You experienced the event. It diminished the choices you had open to you. You chose. You then, explained the choice you made. Most people used deceptions, distractions, or disillusionment to explain their choices and their subsequent behavior. Shelving is the opportunity to examine your narrative—the explanation for your choice—without the shame and defensiveness that does not recognize your diminished choices. This opportunity also recognizes the experience, whether trauma, fraud, fantasy, or victimization that diminished your choices.

An example may be helpful. If you grew up without a father figure in your home, you missed this interaction. No matter what other advantages you experienced, let's say that you longed for your father's presence and guidance. In your fantasy, his presence would have been wisdom in times of questioning and comfort in times of emotional need. When faced with your first love, you see your choices as either lose him or give in to your love's unsustainable demands. When faced with negative consequences, you explain that your father's absence left you vulnerable to a misunderstanding of love behavior.

The trauma is the longing for a father. The diminished choices offered a false choice to either be loved or to lose love. The narrative explains that your father's presence would have meant wisdom and comfort for you.

Our first consideration in shelving is to address the fantasy created in your narrative. You have some sense of loss from your father, but that is not a justification for your choice. It is an explanation for the diminished choice set. With the former, the solution would require the return of your father. With the latter, the solution is to increase your choice set.

Once we have an outline for increasing your choice set, our next step in shelving is to address the fantasy in the context of your relationship with your father. Knowing that the status and character of your relationship with your father is not an acceptable justification for your action, you now have the question of what to do with that relationship. Arriving at this question, "What do I want to do with this relationship?" you have completed the mental component of shelving. The physical component is next.

A Note on Sexual and Secret Trauma. For those items that need more security, place the notebooks of this exercise in a mental lockbox, and place the lockbox on the shelf. As a mental practice, this emphasizes the importance of not giving in to guilt, allowing it to become shame. The experience still needs to be organized and shelved. You must call it out by name. But, the lockbox allows you to understand that the experience does not need to stay on display. You control how it is viewed. There is no need to be defensive or aggressive concerning this notebook. The experience is recorded and useful to you because you make it useful. It is important to acknowledge that it is there, but to seal away all but the elements that remind you of your resilience, your power, and your ability to write your own story.

Following is a presentation of each of the characteristic types of experiences you may have encountered that require mental shelving. Each has a characteristic fear and impact on your narrative.

Shelving Trauma with Information

You experienced trauma. Your innocence, your trust, your expectations for nurture were violated. You wonder if you could ever trust again. You fear opening yourself to a relationship or experience that feels real, and abruptly awakening to it revealed as a sham. You also fear setting your standards too high to reach and too low to weed out the pretenders. You are left unguarded and unsure, ripe for predatory interactions.

Overcoming is a choice to take your power back. From now on, you make your choices based on information, not just your reaction. It was never acceptable to engage your primal instincts alone in decision making. Healthy decision making requires engagement of both reason and emotion. Many like you have denied that feelings had anything to do with their decision. The focus must be on the information. Not a simple attempt to objectify, but an openness to being questioned about the process used at each of the decision points. This transparency will expose your process and resist the cover up and silence of shame.

Shelving Fraud with Competence

Vague praise and 80% achievement have left you with the knowledge that you have more to learn. You have been told that your work was good enough, but that leaves you vulnerable in that moment when you fail—when your best is not good enough. You fear this moment as a moment exposing you as a fraud and a charlatan. The 20% that you never mastered will come back to haunt you.

Overcoming is a commitment to competence rooted in help-seeking and access to mechanisms. Your chief resource is people. Help-seeking may initially be difficult because of the fear of rejection and the admission of your need or sharing of your ignorance. Yet remember, no one succeeds alone. No one knows all. Your admission of ignorance is the first step toward gaining both help right now and increased competence for the future. Access to the mechanisms refers to an ability to see behind the scenes of social life. It is to understand what forms the social structures and decision points of your daily life. When you access the mechanisms, you see interactions and choice as opportunities and influence.

Shelving Fantasy with Legacy

You don't want to forget about what you have lost, especially when it is a person you loved. But many create fantasies beyond the truth of the person. "If they were here…" fantasies only stifle your responsibility in the here and now. The fantasy also diminishes your impact on the future. You fear losing the memory of the person as if your obligation is to commemorate their life through rehearsal and embellishment of their legacy. You have limited what is possible in new relationships and new information holding on to the lessons they were able to complete before they left.

Overcoming is to realize that your honor of them is the legacy you create beyond their contribution. Building upon what they made possible is your task. Rather than the incomplete phrasing of "if they were here…" that only recalls their wisdom, completely express,

"if they were here, they would continue to grow, learn, and challenge the status quo."

Realize that they would want the same and more for you. Realize that life is your opportunity to provide that and more, bolstered by the uniqueness of you, for future generations.

Beyond Playing the Victim

Information, competence, and legacy have in common that they are not things that were done to you. They are what you engage in order to make sense of your experiences. Now, rather than reacting, you can be proactive shaping the world through your own intentional design. Yours is not a backward facing reliance on the past, but an informed, proactive, intentional impact on the future.

Shelving works because you **organize your experiences** so that you can sort out the meaning that is available to you. These are lessons that demonstrate options, opportunities, and consequences. If you learn from those lessons, you expand your awareness. Shelving allows you to **remove the threat to your health** represented by your reactions to your experiences. It was never the experiences themselves that threatened you, but the hindrances, mistakes, and obligation your guilt motivates forming the basis for shame. Shelving also creates the basis for you to **apply lessons to your life moving forward** rather than attempting to address the past. Preoccupation with the past can have you searching for rescue rather than creating a foundation for sustainable risk. Remember, successful life is not about the experience of never failing again. Successful life is about risking on your own terms, and finding joy in the outcomes whether lesson or reward.

Addressing Each Item: The Physical Component

The shelving analogy organized and parsed your experiences into workable notebooks. The process of addressing each item now on the shelf is physical. **The Letter Method** is a proven technique. With this method, your task is to write a letter to the person or thing that represents your experience. The letter has a standard format that coincides with the process of healing and relationship repair. The goal of the process is to get the feelings outside of your mind and onto the paper. Many find this process to be therapeutic. It is also a revealing indicator of the level of resolution you feel in regard to the relationship. Inability to write the letter often signifies a level of denial, suppression, or fear that requires more mental shelving work.

An incomplete letter often indicates a hesitance and shame about calling the experience by its true name. This hesitance can usually be overcome by reviewing the options available to you. The resulting letter can be buried, burned, or bequeathed. Buried refers to putting the letter away as a keepsake--useful as a reminder keeping you from falling into the same trap again. Burning is literally setting the letter on fire or throwing it into a fireplace. This is useful to signify the dissolution of a relationship or dispense of a relationship that is beyond (or unhealthy) to repair. Bequeathing refers to the act of giving the letter to the person to which it is addressed. Bequeathing is done according to a process. First, you read the letter to the person. If they do what you require, you can destroy the letter. If they refuse to do what you ask, and you want to pursue the relationship further, you ask a mediator to explore the letter with you and the person. If they refuse this opportunity you may bury the letter as a reminder of their refusal to consider your feelings.

Standard Letter Method Format. This method is important so that you do not create your new choice architecture and backstory as a reaction. Create the new choice architecture as a proactive expression of what you desire. The letter method is written with three sections. In the first section, you describe the situation as objectively as possible. In the second section, you describe your experience and your feelings. In the third section, you outline what actions would need to be taken in order for you to forgive and move to reconcile the relationship.

Writing Your New Backstory

Rather than rely on the past that you experienced, consider a past that would open your options and be stable enough to allow you to risk. As opposed to fear of what will happen, worrying about what you will lose, consider a past that provides for your basic needs and enables your heart's desires.

Your thoughts dictate your words, and they support creative action. Your motives play out through the people, emotions, and situations you attract. This is the self-fulfilling prophecy of your approach to interactions.

The universe is more energetic than you may realize. If you place your flow of energy toward a certain thought, you will move toward that reality both consciously and subconsciously. Writing a new backstory releases your energy from the requirements or set-up of your past. A new backstory frees you to focus on thoughts beyond what your history suggests as possible. These thoughts order your energy, attracting health and well-being.

Your new backstory has four components. The components are meant to provide you with a clear foundation for your planning, risk, action, and explanations. The backstory follows a typical origin story model similar to what you may find describing your favorite movie character. But, rather than focus on your characteristics, this backstory focuses on your guardians, personal relationships, and experiences you have on recall.

Guardians do not replace your parents as the greatest influence in your life, but we add in guardians that have taken an interest in your progress. These guardians would have bought gifts for your birthdays, and invited you to events exposing you to more than your typical experience. They would be available for counsel and a second opinion when you had important questions. If you make a mistake, they are understanding, and challenge you to explain. They know and call out your attempts to bait and switch, always encouraging you to stand up and accept the consequences for your choices. Many of the clients I have worked with choose a guardian who represents a financially successful celebrity. Oprah Winfrey and Bill Gates are common examples.

Personal Relationships include peers and mentors that you can call for advice and perspective. They have been where you want to go. They have experienced the failures and the triumphs that are common to your station and your aspirations. They were present at multiple times in your experience, and remind you that they have your back. They push you to volunteer and challenge yourself to move beyond fear. They call you on your weak rationalizations and cop-outs. Clients typically choose relationships from among people they grew up watching on television or those whose music they grew up listening to. Will Smith, Beyonce, or Phylicia Rashad are common choices.

Experiences include moments of great inspiration, clarity, or opportunity. Remembering these moments remind you that you can reach new heights because of the heights you reached in the past. You can risk because you seize opportunities, and you have always either learned or gained in the process. Experiences show you the truth of who you are and the inevitability that the truth of others will always come to light.

Typical experiences include "the time I visited Oprah," or "the time Warren Buffet took me to lunch." The point is that your backstory motivates, but also makes reasonable any action that you can think of. Rather than recoiling in fear and second-guessing your ability, you are able to mine your backstory for courage and the assurance that you can take a chance.

Your Potential for Action. Now, it is a choice of goals and creating actions. No more excuses and discouragement. It is not about having the physical resources that your backstory suggests. It is about realizing that the mental and emotional freedom, even the expectation of positive outcome is the difference between the former you and the current you equipped with a new backstory.

Distinguishing Between YOU and NOT YOU

How do you keep it real? You share within a diverse community that challenges your principles. You cannot "overcome" YOU. It is more productive to learn to use YOU sustainably rather than the frustration of attempting to change YOU. A number of habits and misunderstandings exist that are NOT YOU. These can be altered. Following is some guidance to help you distinguish between YOU and NOT YOU.

Defining YOU

YOU always find yourself in the same situation, pulled in a certain direction, engaged in a certain activity or thought pattern. You want a certain reality so bad that you can taste it. You breathe desire out, and wish desperately that you could inhale it as reality. Despite time, distractions, and your best efforts, this desire will not leave you. You find yourself faced with the same lessons over and over again. This is because your life events, your environment, your relationships, your choices, and your perspective have resulted in a certain meaning for your life. This is YOU. This signals your purpose. To change these realities concerning you is to cease to be YOU.

For example, you may "love hard." Once you invest in something or someone, you find it nearly impossible to rid yourself of the inclination to help or to be of some service. You can attempt to bar them, avoid them, refuse the activity, or otherwise redirect yourself, but the pattern always returns.

You must communicate plainly to yourself, "Your life events, your environment, your relationships, your choices, and your perspective have resulted in YOU MUST GIVE." Rather than warring against this fact, explore your motivations, learn about your desire to give, and construct ways to sustainably satisfy that desire.

Identifying NOT YOU

"NOT YOU" is clearly evident in outcomes. But, you may be surprised to know that the outcome is not evidenced in the guilt you feel. Some of that is a lack of understanding YOU. The outcome evidence is the lack of compatibility between the actions, the results of your actions, and your goals. Quick fixes, immediate gratification, words and actions without thought, or betrayal of your future are NOT YOU. Temporary fixes or approximations of satisfaction like drug use, panhandle donations, or over-indulgence are NOT YOU.

For example, your exploration revealing that "YOU MUST GIVE" means that you are motivated to share in relationships. You have researched and learned that one sustainable way to consider "giving" is the economic transfer described in reciprocity. Your task therefore is to construct reciprocal relationships—meaning that any proposed "giving" on your part must carry a clear message about what you want in return. If the return is not certain, you must state clearly to yourself, "That is NOT YOU."

Utilizing YOU

It is YOU to satisfy your primary drives—those insistent desires. Just because you have met them unsustainably in the past does not mean that they should now be considered bad, evil, or NOT YOU. You don't have to change. Your sustainable option may be to accept and integrate this reality about YOU.

Change is possible if that is the choice you want to make. My point is that changing YOU would transform you into a new person. Seek help, because few are able to complete a healthy transformation alone. For those who want to attempt this, I suggest that you enroll in a boarding institution like a university, the military, or a study abroad experience. You must replace your daily routines, your environment, your relationships, your choices, and your perspective if you hope to change YOU. Before you make this choice, take time with a counselor to explore what the current you, even with what you consider flaws, adds to the world. Consider what your closest friends appreciate about you. Consider what the world would be like if that YOU were not present.

I offer another way: accept YOU and choose to satisfy YOU sustainably. In your exploration, ask yourself tough questions. Develop clear, logical, actionable answers. Find out what YOU really want. What is the reality that would make YOU happy for the long term? No matter if it seems impossible. Honesty about YOU is so much more important.

In your research, learn new words and complete vocabulary with which to communicate and understand YOU. If giving, being needed, satisfying others, or proving yourself is YOU, economics provides a useful lexicon: exchange, reciprocity, production, distribution, consumption, cost-benefit, loss-leader, investment, efficiency, supply/demand, markets, growth, and more. If wanting to be rewarded, wanting safety or any derivative of needing from others is YOU, physics offers a useful lexicon: principle, rules/laws, inertia, matter, force, attraction/magnetism, mechanism, dynamics, and more. Use these words to inform and construct choice architecture that result in sustainable movement toward your expressed goals.

For example, you have admitted to yourself, "YOU WANT PRAISE." You have explored that this means that you want to be respected for your contribution. You are disappointed when your contributions are not valued at a level of praise that meets your standards. You learn that rules (in physics) provide a foundation for calculations and assumptions about the world. You construct a framework with rules to govern your choices toward satisfying your need for praise.

One technique as a rule: Two separate categories of contribution exist in every transaction. *Disposable* are contributions that are founded in your excess or time YOU specifically identify to give away. *Sacred* are contributions that relate to the things YOU value more, and the time and other resources reserved for those you care most about. Contribute first out of your excess, the disposable contribution that you have already decided to give away. Never allow yourself to gamble with what is sacred. And, never beat yourself up when your disposable is not revered as sacred.

This rule allows you to appreciate praise that you receive from giving of your disposable time, like volunteering. You give time that you have set aside. Do not give away things that you will miss when they are gone or that you cannot replace. Do not assign fault to yourself when those contributions of time are not valued. Note that you will feel the most consistent praise through "sacred time" spent with family and valued friends. They naturally and actively demonstrate appreciation for you.

Explore YOU. Learn to articulate YOU. Construct sustainable ways to satisfy YOU. Stop punishing yourself over things that are NOT YOU.

You Can Be Wrong

The chief of these principles is that you can be wrong. You continue to learn and grow. You continue to redefine. Admitting that you are wrong allows for additional options. It is admitting to the truth. Denial keeps you from the options of self-correction. The basis of dissonance, motivation for defensiveness, origin of deception, reason for distraction, and cause of eventual disillusionment is denial. You don't develop the roles, responsibility, foresight, and insight that supports healthy, informed choice behavior by denying that you make mistakes.

It was the Will Smith and Jaden Smith movie *After Earth* that promoted the quotable, "Danger is very real, but fear is a choice."

Throughout your life, you are faced with different variations of the same FEAR theme. I am interested in the diversity of the choices you are able to review before fear diminishes options. I want to know how many of those options you feel empowered to put into practice before fear tells you to think again. I submit to you that all of these decisions are a choice between sustainability and unsustainability—the opportunity to support your future goals or the chance to thwart your progress. Let us take two common fears to task. I will describe each, the choice involved, and the way to choose sustainability when faced with the fear choice.

Fear of failure is that stifling inclination often misdiagnosed as procrastination or perfectionism. The identifying difference is that fear of failure results in NOTHING being submitted. When gripped by a fear of failure, you hold out even past the deadline. Your logic is, "If I don't risk while the expectations are high, I can ride the diminished expectations of a late entry." If you "fail" with these circumstances, you can rationalize that the failure was not yours completely, or "I didn't fail. I just didn't compete."

The danger is real. You could be ridiculed or otherwise embarrassed. Your product could be judged as poor or rudimentary. You could learn that your skills are not as high when compared to others or evaluated by experts.

Yet, the choice is to see your goal as that of a learner. Each risk is an opportunity to learn...about your critics, about your competition, about your craft, and about yourself. No matter the outcome, you benefit because you learn. You have additional knowledge to inform your next production cycle.

Fear of being alone is that insistence that you engage and remain in unhealthy, unproductive, even hurtful relationships. Often misdiagnosed as loyalty and commitment, they are obvious to outsiders because they leave you bitter, anxious, defensive, and otherwise ill-suited for healthy interactions. You are passionate in your criticisms of the other person. You are quick to identify flaws, lies, slights, and validated suspicions. But, when the suggestion of new directions is made, you begin the defense, "But, he/she is a good person."

You only have one, maybe two, people in your life that you feel you can truly count on. You live in a constant panic worrying that they will one day pass away. You know it is inevitable, but you thank heaven each day that they remain.

The danger is indeed real. You may have to endure some heartache in your life time. As surely as you find love, you will experience hurt. Those that you count on most may fail you at one time or another.

Yet, the choice is to realize that life is reciprocity–not only what you can receive, but also what you can give. A healthy life is not just about keeping yourself in familiar surroundings and clinging to familiar friends. A healthy life includes an inventory of what you offer to others, how you engage the world, and how you build community. As you participate, you can never be alone. Your authenticity will draw others to you. Your engagement, your shine will encourage others to share their brilliance such that the darkness of loneliness never falls.

The Common Thread

What both these have in common is what all ego defenses have in common. You are wired to first defend yourself against what you sense to be attacks on your person. The perceived attacks can be physical, emotional, intellectual, or otherwise. You defend instinctively as if to protect yourself from death. And, therein is the choice.

The danger of disturbance, the challenge to your ego is real. But, to fear death, to judge yourself by your product, to reduce yourself to a moment's contribution is a choice to be selfish...unsustainably selfish.

The greatest freedom, the most effective weapon waged against fear is to deny the ego its safety. In other words, risk being wrong. Try something you are unsure about. Trade in your need to be right for a desire to learn something new. Instead of protecting your ego, protect (and optimize) your physical body, your mental acuity, and your intelligences. Explore a place of certainty about who you are and what you can contribute to the world. Identify your sustainable impact on others. This is sustainable selfishness: to be healthy enough to offer yourself in service to others. Because danger in this world is very real, but you can make a difference if you so choose.

SECTION IV: OVERCOMING BARRIERS

CHAPTER 13
BECOMING YOUR BEST

Leadership: The Final Fear

I live to overcome fear. I examine myself often. I am perfect. I know that because I learn and change when faced with new information. I am well aware that perfection maintenance stimulates a choice between growth and self-protection. I was challenged with such a choice as I was called to a new leadership position. Two fears surfaced that I would not have guessed were applicable to me. That is the nature of the non-dual openness to maturity. You will be challenged to choose becoming rather than safety. Your learning will ask you to move rather than remain in familiar comfort. I offer my two lessons to you because, upon reflection, I believe them to be the most recurrent challenges you will face as you increase your territory, responsibility, and influence. They are the core challenges of leadership and becoming your best.

First, perfection is a brutal, unforgiving standard. You cannot conquer it, and it rarely rewards your excellence. This is only because we typically define perfection by our achievement. Our version of perfection often seems to insist on rightness and flawlessness. We lose focus on excellence. We then, begin to resist failure. No longer a presentation of our best selves, we succumb to protecting the reputation of our perfection. This is perfectionism—the fear of failure.

This perfectionism can become so core to your fears that you create a lifestyle of self-protection to suppress the fear. You cannot see the fear for what it is until you are in a position of leadership. Challenges to your leadership are needed in order for you to experience, learn, and potentially overcome this fear. These deeply integrated fears threatened to keep you from achieving your next level of success. You have been honest with your hurt, but to get to the next level, now you must overcome your fear. **You must refocus on excellence rather than working to build or maintain your reputation.**

Second, overcoming the knee-jerk reaction of self-protection will challenge your worldview and definitions of self, others, and relationships (the interactive effects between self and others). It is at once the realization that leadership is not about you, while leadership simultaneously depends upon you. Though you are consonant, integrated, and consistent in thoughts, behaviors, and being, a specific dissociation is needed.

Competence in the POSITION is the solution. It is competence based on a new worldview that supports your personal and active engagement, communication, and supervision of others while simultaneously removing your ego from the equation. **You must disassociate the position from your person-hood.** "They should know better" and "They know what they are doing wrong" are not leadership quotes. Neither is, "They are mad at me" or "They question my value."

My Greatest Fear and Yours

I have a fear. I now know that it is my biggest fear. At least, it used to be. Chances are that you have this fear too. I know where it comes from. The good news is that you can overcome it. The greatest fear is the fear of failure. But, before you say, "Oh! I know that one. I have worked through that," or even more unsustainable, "I'm working on that one," let me ask you a question. What do you do when someone accuses you of not knowing what you are doing? Common responses:

- I'll show them because they don't know me.
- They'll learn because they don't know me.
- Forget them because they don't know me.

A leader does not have any of the options above. Realize that two things are wrong with the statements above. First, any option that leaves your team without knowledge is not a sustainable one. Second, failure in leadership is never about YOU as a person. Failure in leadership is about your competence as a leader. It is about leadership regardless of who the leader is. You cannot lead everyone. Some people are not able to follow. But, competent leadership means that you can communicate openly, decide with integrity, and plan transparently.

Revelations One: Perfection Requirement

You fear being held to a standard of perfection. Overcoming this, you will resolve into the best leader you can be. It is freeing to be wholly human and required to be perfect. You may not think so because of the feelings attached to being questioned. But, when you remove the "How dare they question the boss" feeling, you have what you have always had for yourself, people requiring a high standard of you.

It is remarkable. I have not met one person who claims perfection, but I have met myriad, tons of people who require perfection of systems, organizations, other people, and me. I walk in perfection. That's not the problem. The problem is that I expected their resistance of their own perfection to support their allowance of my mistakes. That expectation revealed my fear.

My fear was neatly wrapped in the truth that relationships make allowances for mistakes. If your loved one has a bad day and snaps, you forgive them after some time. But, I want you to learn what I have learned. Relationship does not change the perception that you must be flawless. Relationship cannot be used to hide your fear of failure. Relationship will never make allowance for your failures in performance. It is not simply that your relationships are lacking in empathy. It is that relationships outside of family as well as inside have outcomes that depend on your competence, capacity, ability, and execution. When you do not perform, a vital piece of the puzzle is missing.

The revelation is that leadership does not demonstrate relationship through engagement and caring. Leadership demonstrates value through competence in the execution of policy in decision making, communication, culture management, and system optimization. In short, engagement and caring are secondary. Relationship is not the mechanism or the goal. It is a potential byproduct. The goal is value. The mechanism is policy practice.

Revelations Two: Leadership Requirement

Leadership will lay bare every fear and fault you have, and challenge you to overcome or quit. I have chosen to overcome sometimes and quit in others. But, I had to disintegrate the concepts of relationship/ humanness/ leadership from allowance/understanding/partnership. I mistakenly thought that losing the ability to express my humanness and fallibility was to lose the ability to understand myself and others. I believed that the disconnecting of my personal feelings from the position was a precursor to dissociative personality. I can now share a new understanding of this with added insight.

Caring. You can hold on to the human while not "protecting" your humanness. You make mistakes. You do NOT know everything. But, this fact should NOT be protected or used as an excuse for failures. Further, making that allowance as a precondition to relationship with others is an illness of self-deception. Self-protection is not caring. Self-care and mental health promotion is caring. But, guarding or engaging in order to reduce your injury not wanting to risk hard feelings, jealousy, and disagreement is not caring. It is self-protection plain and simple. You must risk, fail or win, learn, and integrate to risk again.

Dissociation. It is true that being one person professionally and another in personal life is unsustainable. Personal-professional value integration is one important key to integrity, authenticity, and success. My additional insight is that dissociation of the *human* from the *position* **IS** sustainable. Impermanence is one name for this truth. Character is revealed in how you execute the duties of your professional position, but you are not your professional position. That means, when people disrespect, challenge, question you in your professional position, they come up against the position. They have little recognition of you. In truth, they can't see you.

I used to feel that this was an affront to my humanness. It was as though they were denying that behind the position, a human exists. But, I have since understood that this was my attempt to stay protected as fallible and therefore worthy of some measure of understanding. Though it may be true that YOU deserve some measure of understanding, the POSITION deserves no such allowance.

In the position, only one directive exists: Produce! If you are in the position and not producing (or if you are producing and others don't recognize or admit to it) you will be criticized, often mercilessly. That's the burden of leadership. Isolation, ridicule, and heresy are par for the course.

Seems harsh, but the resolution is more humane than some have resolved. Moving free from fear offers the opportunity for a stance that is not defending, but communicating. Not seeking allowance, but outlining the vision. Not apologizing for mistakes, but rejoining solutions. The position is not human, though you are. The attacks are not against your humanness, but they are against your competence in the position. Solution: Get Competent!

Resolutions

I offer four suggestions for the would-be leader who realizes her fears:

1. Decide whether you will **overcome your fear or quit** to utilize energy elsewhere. There is no shame in realizing that leadership is not for you. It does require some complex introspection, and awareness of the energy of others. You may determine that the rewards are not worth the energy costs. Yet, this decision is not about losing would-be friends. It is about stepping up to an opportunity and performing competently in a position of responsibility.

2. **Communicate without the expectation of trust**. Leadership is not a matter of trust. It is a matter of each person's decision to lead within their area of influence or to blame in their area of influence. That decision determines the relationship, not any concept of trust. Your job is to inform that decision with the best, most timely information. Rarely does an individual within an organization disengage. Most often, they influence with purpose (sometimes passively) to lead and progress or

blame and find fault. This is their choice, not your failure as a leader. It is character revealed.

3. Seek to better understand and **operate the culture you lead** within rather than seeking only to connect with persons. Leaders can have great relationships with those they lead, but this is not a requirement. The resistance to follow your lead rests in the perceived relationship between your directives and the policy. The gap between the two--the how, moving from one to the other--is culture. Know both explicitly if you hope to shrink the gap and reduce the learning curve. You can only change the culture once you intimately understand it. You cannot change it by fighting against it. You change it by intentionally operating it.

4. As an intrinsic and persistent value, **adopt optimism rather than possibility**. My favorite quote is, "The universe is rigged in your favor." The quote speaks to optimism, but also to a persistent sense. The universe is more than just favorable. It's rigged. That means that there are no mistakes. As a new friend says at every opportunity: It's all good! It can be good as you continue to learn and build competence. It can be great as you apply that competence in leadership.

These four work when your fear threatens your leadership. They encourage a choice. They provide a strategy. They provide an expectation of success. You can accept the position or don't. You still lead.

System Construction: Chess & Choice

Realize two truths. You influence the choices of others. Your current choice impacts your next choice. Think of your world as a chess board and each human interaction as a separate chess match. Your success is tied to your effective use of your pieces, your awareness of the game being played, and your ability to influence the choices of others.

THE PIECES. Knowledge of self is the primary tool for success. You must learn authenticity. Know that you are not bad or good, your actions are neither. You exist. That is enough, not requiring any additional qualification. You have goals. Your actions are sustainable toward those goals, or they are unsustainable toward those goals.

Use of self is the second tool for success. You know what you are capable of. You know the information you need, or at least you know your limits. Place yourself in situations that fit your ability. Seek out and learn what will expand your ability.

THE GAME. Learning and self-development are the elemental constructs of wisdom. Learning is an increased ability to competently share information. Self-development is an awareness of the impact you make on the world around you. The game you now play is varied, but it is predicated upon your ability to combine these elements toward the expression of wisdom through the creation, promotion, and maintenance of purpose, excellence, and action. Success is the sustainable expression of wisdom. Enduring purpose is called forgiveness. To forgive is to realize a larger purpose. Enduring excellence is called perfection. Sustainably, perfection is the pursuit of excellence. Enduring action is called social agency. Action observed is termed a movement—socialization and mobilization of individual agents into a corporate body.

Purpose

Excellence

Success

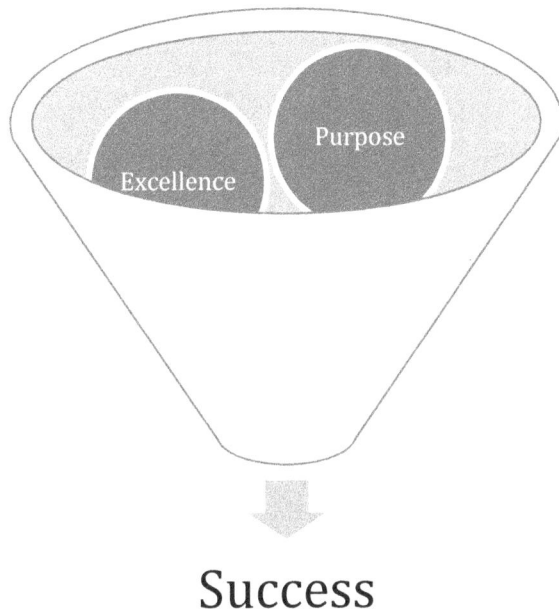

Wisdom in the current game hinges upon health, education, faith, entrepreneurship, and family. **Health** is the one equalizer. Without health, any system will eventually cease to function. Physical health and mental health are intertwined. No medicine can reverse your willful destruction of your health. The discipline you display toward health is exemplary of the discipline you are capable of in production.

Education challenges you to create. No matter the degrees or accolades, you are judged by what you create. Creativity requires a product. Seek to create as a continued expression of curiosity above seeking accolades.

Faith teaches you to risk without having seen the future. Trust is more than just expecting something to happen. Trust is a calculation based on inputs and natural law. Endeavor to coordinate the inputs along with positive expectation, and quality is the expected result.

Entrepreneurship reminds you to seek out markets for your creations. Your choice to participate in community creates value. Your contribution both encourages another, and represents a piece that is needed for the whole.

Family is your model for collaboration. No matter the intention of the other, you can interpret every action as motivation for your success. Nothing you accomplish is accomplished alone. Knowing this will enable you to seek out and connect in supportive collaborations.

INFLUENCE. Social capital is success. The goal is to engage sustainably with others in reciprocal relationships. Therefore, the evaluation should center in whether social capital is gained or diminished. Not a simple lack of burning bridges, but a continual building of bridges that result in new knowledge, relationships, products, and new markets.

Agency refers to the ability to create change. If you do not see what you want the game to be, change the game. More specifically, change the rules of the game.

Understand that the institutions that represent the status quo are groups. Those groups are made up of individuals. You could attempt to change each of the individuals, but human systems teach you another lesson. Those individuals are susceptible to the rules of the game. Focus on changing the rules. You create new institutional mandates. You change the game, and the individuals begin to move in different ways. You determine the needed changes through implementation of your BEST.

Introduction to your BEST

Search for the Real Challenges

Before we can identify the solutions, you must first open up to your core need: to self-protect. You want to believe the lie of self-sufficiency and fearlessness. You even recite the misconceptions. Not only because you were misinformed, but because denial of vulnerability feels powerful in the short-term. You rehearse denial rather than exploring new options because denial distracts you from challenges, isolates you from those to whom you would have to give account, and insulates you from the truth that the responsibility is yours.

There is blame enough to go around. You have been misinformed and systematically silenced by the requirements of polite society. But, it is a waste of time to wait for mis-informants or polite society to accept blame. Your parents and other influences, your experiences and trauma have saddled you with complexity, but it is YOUR responsibility to change the calculus and create success beyond what you were taught. You succeed by solving the equation:

SOLUTION:

$$\text{\sout{Supports}} * \frac{Success}{\sout{Trauma}} = \text{your } B+E+S+T * \textbf{Supports}$$

RESULT:

$$\text{Success} = \text{your } B+E+S+T * \textbf{Supports}$$

Overcoming Trauma in order to live within your Success requires Supports. Now that you comprehend the need for Supports, you must relearn your B.E.S.T.: Boundaries, Equifinality, Structure of Transaction, and Transactions. In your former understanding, you diminished your capability so that it fit better with the Success that you saw as possible. That level of Success was diminished by Trauma. Now with Supports reducing the impact of Trauma, Success returns to its prior level. You may be intimidated even while recognizing the Supports available to you. This is a common experience when your B.E.S.T. has been diminished. Re-learning your B.E.S.T. reconstructs the capability, increases your capacity, and supports sustainability. The result is that you experience your BEST self.

It is you who needs to gain the power and perspective to create competence. You must face up to vulnerability distinguishing between true danger and your tendency to protect your ego. You must take on the adult responsibility to discern relationships based on high standards and your goals in the context of your success.

BOUNDARIES

The need for boundaries often presents as "trust issues." You feel that you struggle with trusting others because of the trauma you have experienced. You were led to believe something, and it turned out to be a lie. Therefore, you are suspicious of everyone. Your first response in interaction is to defend yourself no matter the context.

I offer that the REAL issue is that you cannot trust yourself. Notice that two things become apparent. If you focus on trusting others, the solution would have to involve them. Somehow the other would have to prove themselves worthy of trust. Re-educating the need as a need to trust yourself enables a more realistic solution. Protecting yourself is wise. Yet, engaging defensively in interactions will result in missed opportunities to connect with supportive networks.

To solve this, you must construct a list of rules that serve to protect your interests and promote your goals. The challenge for most is not in creating rules. You will typically find it easy to create a list of protection rules, but you will typically find it difficult to construct a list of risk rules. Let us discuss examples of both.

Protecting your interests requires that you have a clear sense of your "buttons." What characteristic situations, personalities, approaches, and more cause you anxiety? What types of interactions move you away from acting as your authentic self? What constraints or limitations push you toward coping rather than engagement? You know why this is. Your coping is a learned behavior resulting from the training you have experienced. You must learn that engagement and competent respect for authority are not at odds with one another. You must develop and rehearse responses that maintain engagement even when your buttons are pushed.

For example, you may have a boss that is overbearing and reminds you of your father. His insistent demands and degrading language make you uncomfortable to the point where you cannot function at your optimum level. "Why is that paperwork not done? I know you are not slow!" He demands walking up to your desk in an intimidating fashion.

"I can provide you with a timeline and report on what I have completed up to this point, but that would take time away from the paperwork I am working on," you may retort.

"Am I detecting some attitude?" He asks as if ready to pounce.

"I am responding respectfully to your question. Am I free to continue my productivity now?" You respond calmly, providing the boss with an easy way to end the conversation. Above all, the point is not to take the interaction personally. Or, more precisely as I often counsel, take it personally and get over it quickly.

Your rules are best constructed with your specific buttons in mind. Some sample rules that may govern **protecting your interests** include:

1. In confrontations, always provide the aggressor with a choice and an acceptable out.
2. Write out a draft response when you are disrespected. Set the response aside, and review at a later time BEFORE sending.
3. Use email or written contact as a primary and follow-up after interactions to ensure agreement and clear communication.
4. In romantic interactions, always ensure equal capability. If it's a date, it is at a neutral location. Have your own transportation.

Promoting your goals has the built in challenge that polite society admonishes you to abhor self-seeking. "Serve others first," they are often heard to say. Upon closer inspection, you will realize that this admonishment fits a specific context. It presupposes that you are in a position of well-being to even consider reaching out to others. You must learn that service and competent goal seeking are not at odds with one another. It is utterly sustainable to outline a set of goals, construct rules of interaction, and engage honestly, intentionally, and even assertively.

Promoting your goals requires that you have a clear sense of what you want. You often filter your desires through a mesh of questions that lead to unsustainable outcomes. Questions like "what is acceptable," "what makes me appear humble," "what do I view as possible," or "what can others comprehend or validate." These focus your attention on vain attempts at social acceptance as opposed to determining your desires. I insist that you formulate what YOU want regardless of the above questions.

Picture yourself having achieved your desire. Ask yourself questions of sustainability: "What behaviors sustain this reality?" "How is my well-being increased in this reality?" "Am I truly joyful in this reality?" "Does this reality fit with my other desires?" Use these questions to examine what you think you want and clarify what you actually value and desire. Regardless of the acceptability, humility, possibility, comprehension, or validation of others accept what you want, set goals, and create your governing rules.

Rules for promoting your goals are best constructed with an eye toward protecting the authenticity of your outcomes. That is, your most important task is to accept only the genuine. Refuse counterfeits of and substitutions for your goal. Some sample rules that may govern **promoting your goals** include:

1. Prioritize honesty and engagement in review of any shortcut or help received from others. If you must lie or deceive to get to your goal, your result will not be sustainable.
2. Prior to making a decision, filter all choices through a review of whether or not the choice fits with your goals. If the choice does not get you closer to your goal, do not select that choice.
3. In romantic interactions, always communicate your end-game—what you want the relationship to develop into. Do not accept seconds, counterfeits, or engage in behaviors that send a different message.
4. In romantic interactions, do not change your requirements in order to satisfy the other person. Realize that a compatible partner will see your "requirements" as acceptable norms, even desirable contributions.

EQUIFINALITY

The need for equifinality often presents itself as "independence." You rationalize that, in life, there are many ways to get to a destination. Doing it alone must be one of the ways. You rehearse with your inner voice, "If you want it done right, you have to do it yourself." Your logic is based on multiple options, but you only implement one option: Your way or no way.

The truth is you are doing it by yourself because of the need for certainty and security. The problem with this approach is that it unreasonably disregards options. It limits your perception of the utility and the potential promise of the options you do perceive. You are often left with an inferior selection choosing between the lesser of two evils. If you allow yourself to explore other resources and relationships, you have more sustainable options to choose from.

You must re-educate this need as a need to discern resources and relationships that provide certainty and security. You have two fallacious reasoning processes related to this re-education. First, you focus on one resource or relationship to the exclusion of others. You say phrases like, "My mother is the only one I can count on," or, "My boyfriend is the only one who really has my back." These sentiments reveal your inability to distinguish between the varied needs of adult life. Support for sustainable choice requires multiple mentors each providing resources—physical, psychological, and emotional—at the moment of need. To rely on a single person for this varied need is to set you up for incomplete support.

The second common fallacy is related to the first. Because you focus on one person, you find yourself mixing romance with the function of support. Romantic partners can support your sustainable choice as well as give you kisses, but emotional support and romance are not the same thing. This causes you to fall into the first category requiring your romantic partner to be everything at the same time. In addition, you seek out and continue—often to the peril of romance—with romantic partners who do not have the skills to support your most sustainable choices. You remain in the relationship because of the semblance of partnership, open exchange, and mutual support even though the options and outcomes are obviously inadequate to the objective observer. You also exhibit an inability to commit in coaching or educational relationships because of a fear of betraying your romantic partners or a fear of "falling for" the supportive individuals.

To solve this, you must learn to evaluate authentic people and leverage relationships. The central concept in both these behaviors is reciprocity. Equifinality is based on the transaction between you and your environment (including individuals, institutions, and culture). In healthy transactions, each party gives and receives. This is reciprocity.

Reciprocal relationships are characterized by giving and receiving on both sides toward the creation of mutual support. It is not only true that multiple ways to get to a success exist. It is also true that a multi-sourced, mutual support system will expand your options.

Authentic people all have something in common. You can **evaluate authentic people** based on clarity, consistency, and transparency. They are always clear about what they value, what they are willing to give, and what they expect from a relationship with you. You may not receive a formal presentation of the parameters of your relationship, but authentic people are transparent about their intentions and what benefit they derive from your relationship. Do not be fooled by this component alone. Some relationships involve authentic people who only support unsustainable choices. They state the benefit they receive, but are less than willing or incapable of articulating their intentions.

Leverage must also be a component of equifinality. In order to **leverage relationships**, you must develop the ability to articulate your values, what you are willing to give, and what you expect from each relationship in which you engage. Your goal is to succeed. That is, you seek to increase capacity, competence, and confidence. Your relationships should support this goal. In addition, they should honor and value what you are willing to give. They must also be willing to give, consistently, what you desire in return. You evaluate your leverage by determining whether it results in movement closer to your goals. Rules to support leverage include:

1. Articulate your values with an awareness of each decision point in the process between where you are now and where you want to be.
2. Allow flexibility in the choice of activities, but ensure that your actions and what you allow conform to your values at each decision point.

3. Understand that you can (must) expect the outcomes and values to be consistent with your desires and allowances toward increased capacity, competence, and confidence.
4. Expect your contribution to be honored and cherished as a complement that builds the whole.

STRUCTURE OF TRANSACTION

The need for structure of transaction often presents as confusion over self-worth or conceit, self-care or selfishness. You wrestle with whether your sense of self is in the sweet spot—not too self-absorbed, yet adequately valuing of self. "Don't boast. Allow others to sing your praises," you hear from polite society. I counsel you to learn that humility and competent, supportive self-evaluation are NOT at odds with one another.

Your real issue is guilt. You are troubled because the requirements you have of others is not the same as the requirements you have for yourself. Whether it is a higher standard for others that they can never seem to live up to, or an unreasonable standard for yourself that causes you to feel like a failure, the feeling to focus on is the guilt. Guilt is a dangerous basis for action. Guilt risks faulty reasoning.

Your standards are unreasonable in the sense that they are not attainable. They are also unreasonable because they lack reason and careful, systematic thought. You have not carefully evaluated a number of options, informed yourself of their expected outcomes, considered the sustainable contribution of others, nor have you chosen the best option. You have settled for the option that was most readily available, and what seemed to alleviate the anxiety for the moment.

You solve this guilt-based, reactionary approach through reasoned reciprocity as your operant structure of transaction. Reciprocity means that each party in the transaction gives and receives. As in leveraging relationships, you must determine what you require as the outcome for each relationship and what you are willing to give. As your operant structure of transaction, reciprocity becomes an evaluation tool. It measures the value of your contribution and the value of each relationship.

Competent, supportive self-evaluation challenges you to consider who, what, and how you want YOU to be. It is an identity question that few address intentionally. Identity begins with your interests and preoccupations. It extends to your motivations and pleasure centers. It rests with your willingness to be wrong knowing that you can learn new things, integrate new behaviors, and grow as a person. The point is to see the value in YOU as the interaction of identity, learning, integration, and growth. Your worth is not a simple accounting of what you have done. It is the value of being—intentionally.

Reciprocal relationships are leveraged relationships—sustainable and complementary. They also have the characteristic transaction of being mutually empowering. You have felt that power from supporters, mentors, and teachers. You may have experienced it in romantic relationships. Even if you have not, the challenge is to comprehend what it means. Reciprocity feels like being understood, accepted, and challenged to be your best self. It requires you to be honest and open to criticism. It often surprises you with the combination. You are at once validated and offended. Validated that your contribution of being is worthy and respected. Offended that the other would claim to challenge you to something beyond yourself. That beyond, is the opportunity and promise of reciprocity—that the two of you could create something more than what either of you could create separately.

Rules that support sustainable structure of transaction include:

1. Create leveraged relationships.
2. Accept you for your interests, preoccupations, motives, and pleasures. Value your identity, learning, integration, and growth.
3. Be authentically honest and open with the other evaluating whether you receive both validation and challenge.
4. If reciprocity is established, identify the product that the two or more of you will produce together.

TRANSACTIONS

The transactions themselves must be consistent with the model of health and transparency reflected in the structure. Yet, the preparation of boundaries, equifinality, and structure of transaction are useless if you do not engage in the interaction. Your experience with transaction is more often a choice to isolate yourself refusing the interaction. You consider yourself to be "private" or "introverted." These may be true, but they are structures of transaction. They are characteristics of engagement. Private and introverted people are not hermits who never engage.

You seek to justify the isolation as risk reduction. In your justification, you are wisely protecting yourself from relationships that have only a partial and incomplete understanding of reciprocity. You are foolishly rejecting relationships that offer reasoned reciprocity that could result in the achievement of your goals.

The truth is that you have not engaged the relationship enough to communicate reciprocity. You fear that you will be rejected. You further err connecting rejection to your worth. You must learn that rejection and your worth are unrelated considerations. Further, your worth is not bound to your interactions. Your worth is bound to the meaning you create.

You solve this by 1) embracing failure and rejection as learning, and 2) articulating YOUR meaning. It is not just that you will encounter failure and rejection. I want you to expect that these will be intentionally presented for your harm and despair. You may have already experienced this tamping down of your natural exuberance at the hands of your parents. They can traumatize you with either unrealistic expectations of perfection or non-existent or pessimistic expectations. Perfectionism tells you that you are never good enough no matter what you produce. Pessimism convinces you that you should not even bother to try.

The flaw in either is that they neglect the point. The danger in both is that they subvert your natural fervor for life and new experiences. The point of anything that MAY result in failure or rejection is to have the experience. To live in that moment. The next moment is learning. To reflect on the experience, improve your approach, or realize the absence of reciprocity. To determine the next experience in light of your goals.

I am not asking you to accept failure or rejection. I am calling you to **embrace the learning**. This represents a fundamental shift in how you see opportunities. Each opportunity is experience and confirmation of your living. No matter the outcome, your joy is in the living. You maintained your rules including boundaries, equifinality, and structure of transaction. And, you executed the transaction. There exists no loss in that. Only experience that fuels your learning, and learning that is the mechanism of a life well lived.

You **create meaning** as a result of how you make decisions, live intentionally, engage in interactions, and respond to consequences. In short, meaning began with your choice. It does not matter what you are given to work with. What matters is the beauty you create from what you are given. Not just the application of your opportunity, but literally the meaning—the WHAT IT MEANS—that you conclude.

So often your greatest mistake is not the faulty actions, but your assumption that their actions were intentionally hurtful. As I have said, they were intentionally hurtful. But, it does you no good to dwell on that or allow it to color your meaning. No matter their intention, your intention, your activity, your production reveals your character. If WE are to ever be honorable and better than we were, YOU must always fashion a life that creates something better out of whatever is handed to you.

Rules for embracing learning and creating meaning include:
1. Make decisions with the expectation of learning as goal and reward.
2. Take steps that communicate your intentions (your best) without fear of the consequences. Allow yourself to be wrong or imperfect.
3. Engage according to your personality. Personality and energy flow is not an excuse to isolate.
4. Respond to consequences as an opportunity to express your character and the standards you aspire to.

B+E+S+T Maintenance

Maintain the sanctity of your rules. Evaluate relationships and interactions authentically. Structure reciprocity in your interactions with others. People will fail you due to their lack of capacity. Others will choose to disappoint you. When this occurs, hurt for the loss, but examine the relationships and learn.

The Point of Overcoming

Your ability to deceive, distract, and disillusion yourself can be used for your benefit. Not fallacy or self-deceit, but a sustainable ability to act within an authentic social role, to act intentionally, and to support progress and community. The problem is that, in your humanist search for purpose and order, you have learned the counterfeits and the superficial vestiges in deception, distraction, and disillusionment. As a result, your temporal orientation is skewed. You are ruled by a past that haunts you. You experience the present as confirmation of the past slights and isolation. You see only a selfish future of getting yourself together.

The single challenge of life is choice to manage your search for purpose and order with the just, progressive, and altruistic expressions of the principles embodied within social cognition, self-efficacy, and community. The challenge is to accept the lessons of the **past**, to live with authority in the **present**, and to influence others into the **future**. This challenge is presented here as a credo for your recitation:

FORGIVENESS: I take responsibility for my choices to seek knowledge, define my social role, and engage in relationships. I approach every interaction as productive. With each choice, I am leaving a legacy that endures with sustainability to my children's children. Honor to those who came before me through my leverage of the resources given. Legacy to those who come after me through my creative being.

PERFECTION: I determine my path. I am a captain with permission, perspective, and purpose. Without apology, I own my desires. I benefit from new information. I act with intention. Whether I believe perfection is attainable or not, my task is to seek after it with each correction, achievement, and experience. I chase perfection. I catch excellence.

AGENCY: I make choices in a way that encourages responsibility and inspires leadership in others. I develop leaders from followers to achieve beyond what I have achieved. I celebrate progress as success. I learn from every outcome. Mine is not to make an impact only. Mine is to inspire and inform a movement.

CHAPTER 14
THE FORGIVENESS CONVERSION

The Forgiveness Conversion describes the process of "dealing with" anger toward the recognition of anger as energy. Energy can be used to sustain or to destroy. If you are to effectively deal with the past and achieve forgiveness, you must become aware of the energy, risk sustainably, and construct a legacy.

A Moment on Anger

After most traumatic episodes, denial gives way to anger. Anger is an emotion characterized by an inconsolable aggression. Not a simple frustration, but the heat and adrenaline that is produced when you are faced with even the thought of your trauma and its chief perpetrators.

If this emotion robs you of energy and saps motivation on a consistent basis, seek help from a professional counselor. It is important to rule out physiological or mental health issues that may be the source of your fatigue.

Some might counsel you to get rid of anger. They may be forgetting what it is like to have anger. Anger is a thunderstorm with strong winds of chaos and crisis. In the midst of a storm of anger, sight is diminished, roadways are dangerous, and everything is drenched with rain.

Your natural tendency to hold back anger creates a reservoir within you dammed by the strength of your will. It can only be held back for a period equal to the force you apply to keep it in check. If the reservoir is continually added to without release, the dam does not have to break. The reservoir will overflow. All that energy will rush through creating a secondary drenching of emotional chaos even after the original storm has long since passed away.

Consider that this analogy is an expression of anger as emotion. The original storm is trauma with its winds representing chaos and crisis. The result could be a loss of electrical power—your feelings of powerlessness. The rain is emotion pooled in a figurative reservoir. The harnessing of this potential and conversion of this emotion into energy are the resolutions of trauma toward the achievement of your continual success.

Reservoirs can be dammed as a way to produce energy. Controlled release of water over waterwheels or turbines produces energy by harnessing the momentum of the water flow to create power for machinery. Your emotions fill the reservoir. They are neither good nor bad. Your forgiveness is the waterwheel. You install forgiveness for you, not for anyone else. The machinery is the mechanism that powers your purpose. Install forgiveness, and power your dreams.

The Achievement of Forgiveness

Forgiveness, as defined by this work, is to move forward toward present choices releasing any obligation to fix, explain, reconcile, or excuse the past. The past just is. The main lesson of the past is that, at some point, you will look back on your current choices as past. Therefore, learn from the past. Make your current decisions such that they will be looked upon as wise decisions in retrospect.

The Forgiveness Conversion is a nine phase project that can be organized into three distinct achievements: Awareness, Risk, and Legacy.

Achievement 1: Awareness

Awareness has three phases: Blame, Intensity, and Direction. I term this achievement as "awareness" because your first achievement in forgiveness is to become aware of the energy you wield. You may not have a handle on controlling its flow and utility, but at least recognize that your emotion is power. Blame encourages you to give fault to those responsible including yourself. Intensity asks you to measure the amount of work involved in your emotion management. Direction challenges you to consider how you might intentionally direct your emotional energy.

Blame suggests that you identify the players in your trauma and recovery. Consider no one innocent, not even yourself. Innocence is lost in trauma. Resilience is what offers to replace it. You cannot change what has happened. You can impact how it ultimately impacts your life.

Sustainable use of blame is dependent on a cognitive restructuring of guilt, shame, and empowerment. Guilt is appropriate. It moves you to act. Shame is stifling. It keeps you frozen. Empowerment is you facing up to guilt, refusing shame, and practicing self-talk that affirms your power. Let go of the shame associated with attempting to deny your guilt and hide behind "innocence" and "powerlessness."

The original trauma may well have been out of your control. You do not have the power to choose and control every circumstance. Yet, you feel guilty. I want you to use that feeling as motivation to look at yourself. See the beauty, the purpose, and the opportunity that lies in front of you. Guilt in this moment is your reminder that you have control over what happens next.

I am not a fan of sharing your trauma, but I am a cheerleader for sharing your resilience—your story of how you overcame adversity. Shame would have you hide as if you are the only one who has experienced disappointment and betrayal. It is simply not true that you are alone. That feeling is loneliness. It is a function of isolation. But, with supportive relationships and a story of resilience, your shame can be named. Your story can open dialogue toward healing. You can realize that you are not alone.

You do not share blame for victimization when you did not know. Yet, refuse the phrase, "I am not responsible." Never give in to say, "I am powerless." Engage in self-talk that affirms your responsibility, your control over the current choice, and your power. The past cannot be changed. Therefore, self-talk in the past tense is not useful. Seize this moment. Speak into this moment. Change your circumstance in this moment.

Realize that you have no control over the actions of others, but you must take responsibility for your actions now. Your actions do influence the actions of others. This is the first step toward reclaiming the power you possess to make sustainable choices that will move you beyond your past. Empowerment is the feeling that you have the resources, structure, and opportunity to move toward your goals in this moment.

Intensity describes the recognition of emotion management as work on your part. You are intent on controlling yourself in certain situations. You want to appear strong and "together." You have goals to accomplish and responsibilities to fulfill. All this requires a large amount of energy. This is energy wasted because you only end up with the illusion of health and well-being. It is not enough to appear strong, and this is not your only option. You can get into the work of resilience. As opposed to spending energy to manage emotions for the sake of appearances, resilience is experiencing and expressing emotions. You gain energy for the sake of growth and development. In this phase, your task is to map your emotional mechanism: your triggers, your medicators, and your healers. Your triggers are the proverbial "buttons" that some people push. Medicators are your typical coping defenses. Healers are the harbingers of your resilience.

Triggers are the instigators of strong emotion. It could be as simple as a song, a smell, or a word spoken a certain way. You are tasked to recognize what it is that signals an additional stressor deposit into your reservoir.

You may find it easier to recognize the straw that broke the camel's back, but this is rarely the trigger. Trace your emotional stress backward to the point at which you began to lose the ability to cope. Begin with your last contented thought. Move forward in your replay until you arrive at the first indication of stress—the first moment in which you had to bite your tongue or redirect your emotion. Once you identify the stressor, seek to understand why it has the hold on you that it does. You may be able to limit, decrease, or remove its power completely through this identification alone. Other times, you may require help to disentangle this stimulus-response connection.

Medicators are often well-practiced. They include the typical ego defenses like denial, projection, and sublimation. They are easy to obtain, easy to implement, and often euphoric in the short term. They also often have unintended consequences that may be long-term, costly, and inconsistent with your goals for yourself. Use of medicators is unsustainable, but often useful in the short term. I emphasize medicators because they are typically a first line of defense when triggers arise. If accepted without intentional review, medicators tend to result in self-medication with substances or poor behavior choices. Your goal should be to move from the utilization of medicator reactions toward more healthy, more sustainable supports. This describes a move from defense to offense—intentionally engaging your support system.

Healers are sustainable supports. They offer a long-term support to your ongoing health and well-being. Actively seek out these supports to replace medicators. It is a great challenge to identify triggers, but once you are proficient in the identification of triggers, you still have the task to train yourself to implement healers. Healers are characterized by reason balanced against emotional states and engagement to create meaning. Rudimentary healers may involve taking your mind off of the trigger with activities that result in self-development. Robust healers actively engage you in reviewing options and predicting alternate outcomes.

Direction is the recognition that aggression can be directed toward individuals, objects, or anything. Direction is the budding ability to control the target of the anger even though the anger, once unleashed, can still be overwhelming to the aggressor. Whether you recognize and are consistent with control or not, become aware of your thoughts even after you have expressed your emotion. This reason adds a new component to your experience.

The coupling of reason and emotion is the beginning of your ability to direct your emotion with mindfulness. You may not be able to completely map the emotional mechanism, but it is enough at this point to realize that emotion comes from somewhere, is intensified by certain triggers, and impacts you, people, and your environment.

Achievement 2: Risk

Risk has three phases: Disappointment, Expectation, and Trust. Know that every relationship will require you to risk. The freedom of choice that others possess creates the reality of risk. The other may let you down, but your responsibility is to be certain that your expectations are not denying the free will of the other. Often, your trauma causes you to replace holes left by failed relationships with new relationships. You expect the new relationship to behave in similar ways to the positives you lost in prior relationships. Rather than experience new relationships without expectations, you layer your needs upon the new relationship often dooming it to be an inferior copy. You miss the unique and exponential improvement that the new relationship may have become. You fail due to your inability to see past your previous experiences. To risk is to remain open to other options beyond what your previous experiences revealed.

All trust requires risk. You can do your homework, but ultimately, to truly trust, you must risk being betrayed. Yet, your self-protection means that you are not often faced with a direct betrayal of trust. You are most often so quick to disqualify trust candidates at the slightest hint of your loss of control.

You cannot require a trust candidate to be at your beckon and call, to satisfy your every whim, agree with you completely, and to associate with you exclusively in order to earn your trust. Refuse the inclination to seek a canary you can cage. Risk and engage with persons you can build with.

Disappointment is the recognition that appointments will be missed, anniversaries will be forgotten, phone calls will reach answering machines, but a commitment can remain strong. You must cognitively restructure considerations of obligation, "supposed to," and passive aggression when evaluating reactions to the other. Relationships between two humans in an uncertain environment are never free from disappointment. But, appointments can be rescheduled, anniversaries can be celebrated late, and phone messages can be returned.

Obligation in your life is most sustainably replaced with purpose. Purpose sets a requirement for competence, confidence, and a clear role. Your task is to make informed decisions compiling, expanding, and reviewing options. You move with courage based on the information and thorough review of options. You define your role based on your interests, skills, and a commitment to learning in the pursuit of your goals.

Expectation refers to the behaviors, process, and results you accept as givens in any relationship. These expectations influence how you approach relationships. Typically, you attempt to replace some loss or need through relationships: Parent, Lover, Sibling, Other. Healthy individuals have many more options for relationships including but not limited to, mentor, teacher, confidant, and cheerleader. Expectations have to be cognitively restructured into negotiations. These negotiations are the work of a friendship under development from association potentially through to confidant status.

Additionally, in order to activate the resilience of those recovering from trauma, poor examples (i.e. leaders who have become sexual partners, or parents that have been abusive, etc.) have to be demonstrated as inappropriate. This is accomplished through clear presentation and agreement on a structure of transaction.

Trust is the recognition that every relationship involves the risk of being hurt. Your concept of healthy trust has to be cognitively restructured to include hurt, loss, and disappointment as normal experiences in the life of the individual. Risking oneself, sustainably, in the pursuit of peak experiences is consonant with well-being. You must create criteria for sustainable risk including, at minimum, boundaries, expected outcomes, timelines, and a commitment to communicate directly.

Trust is an exercise in determining where risk is sustainably placed and where it is recklessly placed. Trust may be violated, but therein lies the truth of intention. When you violate trust, you are communicating that you are not trustworthy. Your task is to listen closely to the communications of those who propose that you trust them. You find evidence in their prior relationships, their characteristic responses and treatment of others, and their reactions to being mistreated themselves.

Achievement 3: Legacy

Legacy has three phases: Intention, Expertise, and Pattern. This is the channeling of your energy into productive activities, engaging in the present with a plan for the future. At this point in the forgiveness conversion, you begin to think less about your present challenges continuing beyond your past. You now turn your attention to your future. Intention explores your intentional action and the impact you propose to have on people and your environment. Expertise is the result of your activity. You learn something and create habits. These worn paths are Patterns that will be followed by others. This final stage of creating legacy completes the forgiveness conversion.

Intention refers to your responsible use of choice and the considerate expectation of outcomes. Most people who reflect and make a commitment to balance emotion and reason begin to recognize a connection between the growth and a need to do something. This need for action is commonly called motivation. Yes. Motivation is the result of growth and maturity. You can use it to push through mundane, repetitive, or arduous tasks. The work gets you to what you really want: peak experiences.

It is this expectation of peak experiences that becomes the focus even beyond the trauma, the need for retribution, or the insistence on revenge. You may have heard or stated, "I will prove her wrong!" This is an example of the rudimentary type of conversion you can experience. The more mature expression is more than targeting "her." It is a recognition that your ultimate goal is to validate yourself. It is to show yourself as worthy of better treatment. It is to show that there was another way to engage with support, information, and opportunity. It is the peak experience that you would provide a more health-inducing path for others. You show that your example proves that anyone can target tasks and execute a plan for success.

Expertise describes the curiosity you seek to quench in moving beyond your past. You still have questions about your role, your options, and your place in the world. You question the strength and resolve of those you have risked with in exploring new relationships. In the Risk phase through Disappointment you learned the need for competence along with confidence and a clear role. Now, through Expertise, build knowledge and understanding such that you can articulate, observe, intervene, even predict. Examine it fully, and prepare to articulate your process to others. This communication to others is the demonstration of your maturity—the ability to train others paying forward your hard-won knowledge, experience, and growth.

Pattern is both the tangible and intangible example that you leave to the world. The key challenge of forgiveness is to recognize that the legacy left benefits those you love and respect as well as those you would rather disrespect. The reality is that when you succeed, when you achieve your best self, few people account for or think to apologize for the harm of their influence. They only seem to have certainty that they were present for the struggle and the triumph.

Some actively summarize, "If you turned out fine and achieved like this, I must not have been a bad chapter in your experience." The most egregious of them may suggest that they deserve to share in your achievement.

The final step in forgiveness is to place your energy and satisfaction into your message, training, and support for the next generation of survivors. Take heart In your present development and peak experiences. Refuse to apply that energy in correcting the delusion of those who have no capacity for authentic, holistic, agentic existence. Move forward further exploring these within yourself and implementing them as an example for others.

CHAPTER 15
THE PERFECTION CONVERSION

You are perfect because you own your faults, not because of the absence of them. Be better each day, but first, be true. – Michael Wright, AKA TheMentor

The adult just simply needs to get rid of some clichés. As a child our parents may have told us that nobody's perfect in order to console us after we did not measure up to our own standard. Back then, we did not have the control, the knowledge, or the ability that we now have as an adult. Now as an adult, realize that perfection is within your reach. Not perfection in symmetry and form, but human perfection the oxymoron of a better world.

Logical Fallacies to Overcome

Let us get a few logical fallacies out of the way first. Are you saying that nobody's perfect because you are not perfect? You are not a lot of things. That does not mean that those things do not exist.

Or, are you saying that nobody's perfect because you have not known a perfect person? You have not reviewed everyone in the world. It is a mistake to generalize.

Are you saying that nobody's perfect because the person you are romantic with is not perfect? That is a personal issue not to be taken out on me. Perhaps the goal should be to support you lover's perfection rather than give up on perfection completely.

Or, are you saying that everyone makes mistakes, and mistakes are proof of imperfection? Now, we get to the root of the problem. This is not just a logical fallacy. This is an unsustainable definition of human perfection. I challenge you to find a definition of human perfection not just perfection without mistake. Find a definition that incorporates what it means to be human. You can call it "your BEST" or "excellence." You can relate it to perseverance or determination. Either is acceptable as long as you do not diminish perfection's momentum with potential statements like "try" or "attempt." To do your best is acceptable. To try and do your best is not.

One of the most fundamental realities about being human is that we can change. We take in information. We process new information. We apply that new information integrating it into our behavior, our knowledge base, and our abilities. You are fully within logic to state that my actions are not always perfect, but to say that I am not perfect is to only evaluate me on my actions in a singular moment. It is like saying that I am only my ability in one moment. You also risk unfairly evaluating me on an action that I do not have the skill or capacity to perform perfectly. My inability would not meet the definition of imperfection. That would be lack of practice.

Of course, your test seems valid because actions speak louder than words. A woman is as she does. Your action demonstrates your character. All these are true, but they describe behavior over time not just in one moment, not just one action.

I'm Perfect AND I Make Mistakes

You cannot judge human perfection in an instant unless you are willing to observe and appreciate the next moment. My test when I catch a student or my child doing something unsustainable is to ask if they recognize the long-term problem with the behavior. I ask if they need help. I invite them to work WITH me rather than attempt to convince me. If they show themselves to be open to help, no harm is done. Learning requires a lesson. If they defend against my help, if they become indignant to my inquiry, if they protest my interest, they resist the lesson and must face the consequences of the choice to isolate themselves.

I do not always have the right answers, but I own my wrong responses. I explore whether I am wrong in fact, or whether my wrongness is the result of your preference. Either way, I accept the lesson, and move to implement that learning at my next opportunity. This is human perfection!

I'm Perfect Because I Learn From Mistakes

"Nobody's perfect" is too often used as an excuse to engage in self-deception. More than conveniently justifying unsustainable action, you resist the conviction to make more sustainable choices. You dismiss motivating guilt, and never engage that unique human ability to grow and change toward a more sustainable existence. This is imperfection, otherwise called stagnation.

The opposite of human perfection has more in common with pride and vanity than it has in common with fault. To say it another way, human perfection is humility. You admit that you do not know it all, AND you accept the learning and self-development required to inform more sustainable choices. Human imperfection is pride, vanity, and conceit. At that moment when you refuse new information, you adopt imperfection.

I'm Perfect Because Only Perfection Judges Me

Often, your denial of my perfection is admittance of your own guilt. Because you would like to assuage your guilt, you seek to relax my standards I set for myself. I refuse to be judged by such a poor standard.

My guilt serves its proper purpose, to motivate change in me. I refuse shame and the search to commiserate. I stand ready to be interrogated, to explain my intentions, and ask forgiveness when I have erred. If you can do the same, you are in a great position to encourage me to do the same.

Why Do I Care About Your Perfection?

You influence others by your actions. You also influence others through what you allow. I refuse to allow stagnation in my social circle. Grow and learn so that you can continually challenge me to grow and learn. The moment we feel we have learned it all, we lose.

Perfection is not knowing all. That's omniscience. Perfection is not being everywhere when needed. That's omnipresence. Perfection is not an ability to do everything. That's omnipotence. Perfection is finding a way to be present in this moment. Perfection is deciding to be more of myself in the next moment than I was in the moment before, and all the while to inspire another to be more authentic in the next moment. Imagine a world characterized by this human perfection.

Absence of Error Fallacy

Darkness can be defined as the absence of light, but light cannot be defined as the absence of darkness. Your perfection cannot be defined as the absence of error. The something that is within you defines your perfection.

Just because nobody IS perfect, doesn't mean that no one CAN be perfect. I had not always been perfect, but now that I am, why would I go back to less?

Perfection is NOT doing everything right. Perfection is not infallibility. Human perfection is deliberating with justice, being truthful about your desires, upright in your dealings, and conscientious about meeting your needs sustainably. It is discerning your intentions and comprehending your motives. Perfection is applying yourself consciously to impact your environment, and sharing in continued development with others. It is having the maturity to stand responsibly in the face of temporal flaws engaging fully, honestly in the human condition. If life does not move you to laugh, you are holding too tightly. Loosen your grip, and enjoy.

Imperfection cannot be your excuse. You are lying to yourself if you make a choice knowing that it delays your goals. That choice, by definition, is not a mistake. When called to account, you cannot use lack of perfection as your explanation. Self-deception is the source of your imperfection, not any mistake.

I agree that perfection is hard to come by. It is true that many do not meet its rigor. My problem is that many use the standard of perfection as an excuse not to try, not to excel, and not to be authentic. Consider that human perfection is not the absence of all error. It is a refusal to intentionally act on new information. Then, to excuse the refusal as an "honest mistake" attempting to forego the consequences. Human perfection is owning up to your choices and their consequences.

Ownership of choice and consequence undergirds two important goals in your life: Authenticity and Honesty. First, it challenges you to be yourself—your best self—every day, intentionally, and without apology. Second, it reframes the reality of your choice behavior. You must admit that the first time may have been a mistake, but repeating the same error is your intentional choice. Your choices reveal your true goals. You have to face the fact that you are choosing who you want to be. If you wanted to be different, YOU would make a different choice.

While implementing ownership, reject perfectionism and the insistence on life and production according to someone else's standards. Perfectionism is an ill-informed attempt to live up to an ambiguous ideal. It is characterized by the insistence that hard work, time, and your focus create value. Perfectionism does not consider the product. This is why it serves only to limit your production. Refuse perfectionism by developing your own criteria including evaluation criteria for the product you will create.

Some accept this view as license to live dishonorably because, "Nobody's perfect. We all make mistakes." They build criteria that are without reason, equity, or responsibility. They refuse discernment, curiosity, and intentionality. These are critical for ownership of choice and consequence. Mistakes too can be evaluated for the degree of ownership accepted. No matter the choice and consequence, you need to be certain of your motivations and your intentions. Your product tells the story. Can you be proud of what you produced? As Vince Lombardi is credited with saying, "Perfection is not attainable, but if we chase perfection, we can catch excellence."

Active Definition of Perfection

Authentic means being you, warts, blisters, and corns. What's in you is what's in you. It just is. It is your burden forged from experience. It is also your opportunity plucked from life's furnace. It is your fear heightened by the unknown. It is also your courage sharpened on perseverance. It is your debt, overdue and overwhelming. It is also your gift, to be used to overcome. Rather than self-hatred and attempts to rid yourself of your desires, focus on meeting your needs sustainably.

Honest means owning up to who you are, the choices you have made, and your potential for action. Honesty is never the bravado of a leap without thought. It is an awareness of self and ability that inspires more preparation, a healthy search for knowledge, and the engagement of partnerships.

Reasonable means awakening to the choices you are faced with and knowing that your choice, your action, makes a difference. You can think through the choices and the consequences. You can predict the outcomes and adjust your behavior accordingly.

Equitable means calculating the costs and making decisions that invest energy toward the greatest return on investment. It is also making judgments based on evidence, long-term sustainability, and community impact. Equity is important in efficient use of energy.

Responsible means standing proudly as your choices manifest as outcomes. It is accepting every experience as an opportunity to learn and grow as a member of a community. It is taking the extra precaution, building on solid instruction, and launching confidently with the goal of engaging in process.

Discerning means awareness of your intentions and motives. You see yourself clearly and gain the ability to see others with clarity. You interpret more than just actions and words. You recognize that every action has antecedent. Every word has a cognitive process.

Curious is a desire to know more about people and their interactions with others and their environment. Healthy curiosity supports the search for information, the observation of people, and the exploration of environments.

Intentional means approaching activity with purpose. Nothing is by accident. Additive with clear thinking, ownership, equity, and responsibility, intentionality means confidence and a connection with your motivations—a defined set of roles.

Congruent means having the same behavior as fits your intentions and thoughts. It is the opposite of hypocrisy. It is not only the appearance of consistency, but it is a holistic synergy between who you are, what you think, and what you do.

Fearless means combining the above traits to challenge and make use of any hesitation, lack of confidence, or prior knowledge. It means intentional, congruent, sustainable action as your only option—the result of authentic, reasonable, honest introspection combined with equitable, responsible investment, along with discerning, and curious evaluation.

The Conversion Behaviors

Authentic

Authenticity asks, "What do I need?" Note the conditioned response you have developed over time based in the pressures, trauma, and attempts to measure up to other's expectations. When you have been your happiest and most free, what were you doing? What desires captivate your imagination?

List Your Desires. The inclination is to be vague and guarded. You may not even fully understand what you want, but start by writing down what you think it is. Then, ask yourself "What do I get out of this?" The inclination is to bury the desires, but I counsel you to feed that inner child, sustainably. The task at hand is just to admit to yourself that IT (whatever IT is) is a desire. Resist the need to determine if it is good or bad. Only ensure that it is true.

Once you identify your need, do not attempt to defend it or explain it. Right and wrong is not the question. The choice is to meet the need sustainably or to meet it unsustainably. The need identifies the choice that lies before you. It is what your pressures, trauma, and attempts to measure up have **CONDITIONED YOU TO BE**. If you can redefine your story, expand the options you are empowered to choose, and produce an alternate legacy, you can meet this need sustainably. The authenticity and sustainability you choose in this moment determines **WHO YOU ARE**.

Honest

Honesty asks, "Who am I?" Rather than attempting to dismiss who you are and become someone you are not, accept that your desires are real. Stop attempting to make your desires acceptable. They are what they are. Accept yourself for who you are. Your desires do not define you though. Your actions define you. Your reflections provide context. The goal is to intentionally choose your actions. Think integration, not change. Your legacy is not tied into your wanting. Legacy describes your impact on others.

Accept Yourself. You are inclined to dismiss your self-analysis at each realization and attempt to make your desires or tendencies acceptable. I implore you to be honest, and accept you for who you are. Desires are your attempts to resolve conflicts within yourself and maintain safety in the world around you. Choices, environment, options, social influences, and biological factors contributed to what you now perceive as your desires.

You desire what you desire. Rather than hating yourself because of it, accept that you are perfect the way you are. Your perfection is to accept you as made in an image of infallibility. Even your frailties and desires can serve a purpose toward improving the lives of others. Even your mistakes can offer lessons of value and resilience. From your example, many can resolve to overcome.

You may have been taught that merely entertaining your nature or constructed desires is wrong. I ask you to suspend the need to assign rightness or wrongness for the moment. **FULLY ENGAGE IN THIS MOMENT** of contemplation prior to action. Become whole knowing that you are not controlled by any random thought. Accept yourself honestly, and lessen the chance that you will **DECEIVE YOURSELF**.

Reasonable

Reason asks, "How can I meet my need sustainably?" Reason allows you to construct a choice model that highlights your power to choose. And, this is what separates you from the animals. You can think through the actions before you make them. You can consider the consequences. Consider the best case, the typical case, and the worst case.

A choice model is a set of principles, boundaries, and structural controls that provide clear parameters for your choices. You maintain the integrity of the principles, boundaries, and structural controls governing your decisions by reasoning through your acceptance of the consequences resulting from your actions. When your desired goals are kept within reach and your principles are not violated, your choice is sustainable—it is consistent with the goals you have set for yourself.

Build Your Choice Model. You have accepted your desires. You have realized that your choices/actions define who you are. Now you must **PRACTICE DISCIPLINE.** Before you can choose the sustainable path, you must overcome the tendency toward taking the "easy way" to meet your needs. The "overcoming" refers to your choice to **MEET YOUR DESIRES IN SUSTAINABLE WAYS**. You must ensure that you define success as maintenance of discipline—a lifestyle of intentionality, rather than a simple meeting of your need. Act decisively. Consider the consequences of action. Remain open to development and growth in your understanding, responding with behavior adjustments in the face of new information. Consider the impact of your choices on your relationships and your environment.

Principles guard your integrity. Boundaries ensure sustainable behavior. Structural controls reinforce your control over the situations of choice. Principles are the truths that instruct boundaries and ethical behaviors. Principles describe how you believe the world works—the relationship between nature and nurture, the connection between action and reaction. The following are examples:

1. Relationships should be reciprocal with both parties giving and receiving.
2. Truth is revealed in action. Any promise must be supported by consistent action.
3. Pain and trauma causes need and reinforces dualism, fatalism, and isolation.

Boundaries are simple rules of engagement. They extend directly from principles. Boundaries articulate principles as behaviors. Articulation of the above principles would extend as follows:

1. Engage only in relationships in which I can freely give and freely receive with a person who both gives and receives.
2. If a person does not show me with action, I will not believe what they say.
3. Resist a view of every question as simply black/white. Consider what I CAN do, not being passive. Engage with my mentors and support system even when I am hurting.

214

Structural Controls are guidelines that you conceptualize to be used exclusively at the decision points. Decision points refer to the actual moment you are faced with a choice. You may have clear boundaries, but if you allow yourself to be placed in a certain situation, you may find yourself acting against your established boundaries. The solution is to steer clear of those situations.

Structural controls include physical environments as well as social situations. Your list of structural controls is added to continually as your influence, relationships, and environments change. Structural controls keep you from falling into or intentionally creating a convenient route to unsustainable choices. Some of my favorite examples include the following:

1. If you have created a conditioned connection between food and emotion, you may be tempted to eat to affect your emotions. Do not keep unhealthy or high calorie-low nutrition foods in your home.

2. If you have created a conditioned connection between safety and male companionship, you may be tempted to allow unhealthy people to hang around you at times when you are the most vulnerable. Do not allow any males in your home after 8pm.

3. If you have created a conditioned connection between unconditional love and sexual activity, you may be tempted to classify all non-physical love as not love. Or, you may seek to engage physically in order to "prove" love. Do not have sexual contact until you have a signed contract of the union and permanency of the relationship.

4. If you have created a conditioned connection between alcohol and sexual promiscuity, you may be more sexually vulnerable when you drink alcohol. Do not drink alcohol when you are or expect to be in intimate situations (i.e. when

you are around people with whom you could conceivably have sexual intercourse).

Equitable

Equity asks, "What costs am I comfortable with and what returns do I expect?" When you are equitable, you apply energy where it is needed for the greatest return on your investment. Identify considerations for evaluating return on investment including evidence, sustainability, and impact. Consider your energy expenditures, reserves and inputs.

Your investments of time and money reveal the goals you hold dear. Up to this point, you have been attempting to satisfy some amorphous qualification of future reward devoid of substance. Maintenance of the façade drained you of energy without fulfillment as a return. When you looked up from your hard work, you observed no change in the world around you.

I offer you another option. It is to feed your inner child toward a set of identified goals. In each moment, at each decision point, choose the direction that supports your goals. The result will be consistent progress toward your goals.

Your "inner-child" must be fed. Comfortable with the boundaries of the choice model, you are now able to engage in activities that once seemed "wrong" or "childish" or "scary." You can now shake the self-talk that reinforces that you are not good at some task. You can give yourself permission to fail, to look stupid, to be embarrassed. You can be terrible at something until you get more practice. You may not have learned, practiced, and integrated the activity, but with investment in the task, you will succeed. If that task stands between you and the lifestyle you want for yourself and the impact you want to have on the world, it must be sustainably conquered.

Determine YOUR approach. Starting with your choice model as the foundation, you must determine your approach to the ethical, moral, spiritual, and political questions around you. Determine the investments that you are willing to make. Your core resources are time and money. With them, you can develop access to people and information. Consider the what, when, how much, where, and under what circumstances you will develop your investments. This is your investment strategy toward achieving your goals. This is your approach to equity.

Now is the time to stop attempting to satisfy a requirement that you did not create. Resist the tendency to determine your investments without considering your need. Instead, outline how you will **SPECIFICALLY INVEST TO MEET YOUR NEED**. Invest your time with a certain expectation of return. Invest your money with a clear path toward your goals and certainty about what the investment enables. Engage people with a structured choice to love you or to love you more. Engage information from multiple points of view.

Responsible

Responsibility asks, "What is the impact I want to have on others?" Life is a process. You must be fully engaged and willing to stand behind your choices. Even prior to any action, you must decide whether you can be committed to this course. Your choices will impact others in various ways. Consider the groups of people from those you hold dear to those you could not care less about. Consider the legacy you leave.

Establish your goals for yourself and your impact on others. Once you make your choices subject only to a question of sustainability, articulate the goals you have for yourself. When faced with a choice, you ask first, "What is my goal?" Second, "Does this choice get me closer to my goal?" Third, "Does this choice in the long-term or the short-term hinder my goal achievement?"

Rather than adhering to some list of tenets outside of yourself, figure out what your response is as a more selfish determination for your own health, sanity, and well-being. Reject conformity, political correctness, and right-wrong dualistic thinking. These constrain your goal setting and condition you toward mediocrity. Replace them with creativity, depth of insight, and determination of sustainability. These **MOTIVATE YOU INTRINSICALLY** and condition you toward self-sufficiency.

Take the time to actually create a list of goals. Instead of saying, "I will incorporate some of the fun things that I like to do." List the actual things you want to do—the activities and tangible achievements. That way, when you achieve them, you can assess the satisfaction you get or don't get from them. If the achievement is not as gratifying as you thought, rethink the goal list.

Discerning

Discernment asks, "What systems and environments do I perceive?" Articulate the options you perceive within the context of the systems you encounter on a daily basis and the environments surrounding you. By knowing your motivations and intentions honestly, you can gain insight into the motivations of others. You can predict how changes within the system or environment may influence your choices. This knowledge helps you comprehend and influence the choices of others. It also allows you to engage with systems and environments that support your goals, while refusing systems and exiting environments that are not consistent with your goals.

Map Your Context. It is important that you see your people, places, and opportunities for what they are. Resist the overly simplistic criticism that you are judging. Judging is only unsustainable when it is unjust—when you are judging with a standard that you are not willing to apply to yourself. **APPLY A JUST STANDARD**—one that you are willing to stand behind and be measured by. Use this standard to evaluate the choices in front of you. See people both in this moment and for what their actions communicate. Determine the energy flow between the two of you. Limit those relationships that drain. Nurture those relationships that feed energy. Value most highly those relationships that are reciprocal.

Do not underestimate the importance of place. Whether it is a spot in a coffee shop or in your home where you get the most lucid thoughts, take that truth into consideration. It could be as large as an opportunity to claim your dream job or as small as an organizational membership, yet you must discern in the same way. Determine whether it feeds energy or drains energy. Invest in those places and allegiances that are reciprocal and progressive.

Curious

Curiosity asks, "What is my expertise?" The contexts that you define are the chess boards upon which you play the game. You must learn about the rules of the game. Search for information, observe people, and explore these environments. The starting point for this exploration is your insight, competence, and informed interests. You may not recognize it as expertise, but consider what you know more about than most of your peers. Consider that topic and capability you seem to pick up more and increasing information about even when you are not intentional about skill building. This is your expertise.

Articulate Your Expertise. This is critical to your perfection conversion because it is the primary contribution you make to the world. Not only is it a key point of interaction, but it is the first opportunity for you to be evaluated by the other. You will experience some level of anxiety and trepidation. But, your task is not about the evaluation. Your task is about the articulation, complete and unfettered, of your expertise.

You do not need to be the most intelligent person in the room. You should know by now that you don't need to know everything. You don't need to know everything even about your interest. You are only to **COMMUNICATE YOUR GENUINE CURIOSITY**. Your engagement and search for more information is the only access credential you require. If you find yourself unwelcomed by those in the group, it is a clear indication that the group is not one you can grow within. If you find support and development within the group, it is an opportunity waiting to be explored. When you find expression, growth, and a giving as well as receiving, count that group as home.

Intentional

Intention asks, "What roles am I willing to play?" Consider the usefulness of collaboration, mentoring, and friendship relationships. Role definition illuminates the pieces on the chess boards and the moves available to you at any given moment. The roles you adopt will constrain you in social situations, so work from authenticity to curiosity to confirm your genuine self. With that foundation, you are able to engage perfectly with others.

Delineate Your Roles. Maintenance of intentionality requires a clear sense of what is expected of you. Rather than allowing others to dictate expectations that you must conform to, actively select environments, people, and interactions that fit with the roles you determine. Said another way, know YOU and consider how YOU impacts and is impacted by various situations and contexts. You may not always know what a situation or context has to offer or what it expects. But, you must always know you. Feel empowered to **TAKE THE TIME YOU NEED TO ADJUST** to new and unfamiliar situations. Observing and considering are not negatives. Use your power of choice, your supports, and your competence to impact the situation accounting for its impact on you.

Congruent

Congruence asks, "How consistent is what I think, what I do, and what I believe about myself?" This is consonance, the opposite of dissonance. Congruence seeks consonance between thoughts, actions, and beliefs especially where YOU are concerned. When dissonance occurs, it indicates that new information is available for assimilation. Determine what needs to be adjusted in order to bring sustainability and congruence back to your experience.

Review your choice behavior and intentions on a periodic schedule. This is one of the major differences between perfection and perfectionism. Perfection allows for growth, change, and integration. Perfectionism attempts to maintain a standard that refuses to take new information, new challenges, and new tools into account. Perfectionism seeks the same praise it has always received however inadequate it is at this current stage of development. Perfection seeks a deeper experience of production rather than praise. Perfection seeks to be inspired to the next level of development.

When faced with decisions, **CONSIDER YOUR DESIRES, INTENTIONS, and POTENTIAL OUTCOMES**. Determine whether they all add up to sustainability for your goals long-term and short-term. If you experience the worst of the potential outcomes, are you able to live with those consequences?

Fearless

Fear asks, "Why try?" **Fearlessness** answers, "I act out of my perfection to create what I want to see in the world." Ultimately, perfection is about creation. Your creation will not always be perfect, but you will always apply YOU perfectly in the pursuit of a perfect creation. This is excellence. Resist fear that focuses on the potential for flaws or poor evaluations. Live within the opportunity to apply yourself and view the consequences. If you fail, you learn. If you win, you build. Either way, you gain.

Answer Fear with Action. Fear is not real, but it sure feels like it is. The important thing is not to allow fear to paralyze you and become SHAME. The best way to address this is to **NAME YOUR FEARS**. Write them down and contemplate their origins. You will find that the fears are rooted in vulnerabilities you know about yourself. You fear that others will become aware of your flaws and judge you somehow unfit. The fear pathway has been well-worn, so you cannot just dismiss it. You have to re-package it and "place it on the shelf." In this way, you can risk without allowing the reality of a past disappointment to tell you the outcomes of a new opportunity. Silence that voice in your head that says, "I know what she will say when I do this," or "Why even try? I know what's going to happen."

You will be challenged to push forward through your fear. You must determine what and the ways you will risk. Go back through your choice model to ensure that you can risk sustainably by following your rules to maintain reasonable safety (not absolute safety), and reach your goals while feeding your desires sustainably. Describe how you will put your to-be-shelved items on the shelf. Detail the actual process and understanding that you are resolving—the contract with yourself. If you have been wronged, what do you require in restitution? If the restitution is provided, what relationship or interaction will result?

CHAPTER 16
AGENCY AS AN ENDURING ROLE

Yes, it is difficult to rise above your training. It seems strange to refuse self-doubt and second guessing. Difficult to refuse political correctness, and respect your gift while the world orders you to conform to something you do not fully understand. It is our gift that made us question our place and seek uniqueness as opposed to conformity. Salvation is to recognize the value of my contribution, to offer my best because I am the only one who can fully express my gift. Said another way, the goal in life is not to "be the best person I can be." That is the DAILY grind of perfection. The GOAL is to influence others to be greater, even beyond my time on earth. It is my responsibility to act with others, to collaborate according to my role, to leave a legacy that speaks to future generations as clearly as my living speaks.

Your Gifts Make Room For You

You believe that the point is belonging. It is not. The point is connecting. Belonging allows you to sit in silence and watch the activities of life unfold. You are not required to participate. In the unsustainable model, belonging is enough. Connecting is a more sustainable model. Connecting requires your active participation. Without your intentional tasks, no point exists. This is the beginning of AGENCY within you, within partnerships, and within institutions.

Within You. The easy part is that your tasks extend naturally from your giftedness. If you do not know your gifts, your first task is to discover your gifts. If you know your gifts, you must develop a vision. Agency is how you make your vision into a reality. In order to ensure that deception, distraction, and disillusionment do not destroy the reach of your vision, you must redefine your world through the filter of universal laws. Whether you come to know them through physics, vipassana meditation, literature, religion, or some other way, the point is that revelation comes with time. Judge yourself and insist that others judge you by the fruit you produce. As you succeed, questions about your methods lose their validity.

Within Partnerships. Life is an opportunity to connect with people who can help you and with those you can help. Connection is not simply a requirement to belong to a central grouping or institution. Connection is an opportunity to partner. Often, older generations connect and provide insight to younger generations. But, the commodity is experience, not age. Sometimes it is a family member or a close relative. But, this generativity can operate outside of blood relationships. The challenge is for you to distinguish between people who are genuinely interested in your well-being and others who engage with you only to validate their choices or institutions. Your newfound sense of agency will give insight into possible partnerships. You make the choice to be in a relationship or to refuse. Just ensure that the outcome of partnering meets your needs.

Within Institutions. Institutions can provide the infrastructure to connect in meaningful ways or they can be crucibles of conformity. Meaningful connection encourages you to be your best, to challenge yourself, and to constructively challenge others. Many ways exist to support this approach. Communication, critique, mentoring, partnership, and more are supported through schedules, standards, technology, and tradition. The beauty is that anyone entering the institution can easily engage because the structure already exists. Often, the message is of connecting and "We'll help you expand."

Crucibles of conformity will whitewash you. They seek to make you a follower. They are unconcerned with your individual gifts. For some of these institutions, the standardization is the result of a lack of vision, infrastructure, and the will to create a culture of supported individualization. In others, the conformity is an intentional limiting of your personal potential. Often, the message is one of belonging and "let us do it for you."

Connecting is more sustainable long-term. In order to make connections, you must offer something of value to others, and expect them to offer something you value. The best of these relationships will be reciprocal and complementary.

Knowledge that Creates Community

You get first choice. You have often chosen the easy route. I encourage you to choose your best in contribution to our relationship. You may not be the expert, but contribute your best.

Imagine if you had the knowledge that could save a life. If you were the only one in the group who had that knowledge, would you keep it to yourself? Suppose that you encounter a choking man near a supermarket samples stand. Onlookers watch in horror as the man clutches his throat gasping in vain for air. It seems that no one knows what to do. The man's wife can be heard screaming, "Someone help my husband!"

You happened to have attended training on the latest procedures for choking adults. You answer the call for help with strong back slaps. When that does not work, you move into position for abdominal thrusts. You compress the man's lungs with pressure to his diaphragm in a thrusting motion. His airway is cleared!

My point is that your refusal to use your gift keeps me from living fully in my gift. You are not just a singer; you have a voice of gold. But, when asked to sing, you refuse. You have such charisma. You can charm sheep out of their wool. But, when asked to speak to a group of teenagers, you decline. I am upset that your refusal demonstrates that you do not see your worth. But, I am angry that you have decided to forego the opportunity to inspire me.

Your opportunities to share your giftedness are your daily responses to the screaming requests of that wife whose husband is choking. Daily and less dramatic, these opportunities are no less important. They not only provide practice for the more public and lauded opportunities. They demonstrate that you are a person that rises to opportunity, and that you realize your impact on community.

Knowledge and Status

Imagine if the person who helped in the choking example above was a medical doctor. It changes your potential interpretation of my point considerably. Imagine that a doctor in the supermarket observes the choking man. Abdominal thrusts do not dislodge the sample from the man's throat. A quick probing in the man's mouth with fingers proves fruitless. While you watch, the doctor asks the man to lie down. The doctor takes the sharp knife from the sample table and makes an incision in the man's throat. The doctor disassembles a pen and inserts it to re-establish air flow to the man's lungs. With the immediate distress overcome, the doctor searches and removes the obstruction.

Let us change up the story to illustrate a point about status. The doctor is in the supermarket just as before. She finds the person choking and begins the cricothyrotomy. Instead of just watching, this time, you engage the doctor and ask, "What can I do?" She is grateful for the help, and has you prop the pen shaft as she secures it with tape, and moves to remove the obstruction in the trachea.

I would venture that onlookers would hold you in similar esteem as the doctor. The difference in the two versions is that, in the second version, you offered to make a contribution. Do not take pride in the celebrity that resulted from your heroism. Learn a lesson that motivates your continued contribution to community. **Even when you are not the expert, you are a potential contributor to collective success.**

You see doctors as having access to knowledge that is unavailable to you. Your inability to find your contribution, your role, causes you to increase your awe of the doctor in the example. You believe that you could never do something like this. What is worse, that belief is enough to ensure that you never will.

Knowledge can create community, but only if you continue to seek to learn. Not learning alone, but also self-development, making your unique contribution to community. In this way, you create community rather than a caste system in which the focus is on gaining power, prestige, and status rather than gaining relationships, exhorting others, and contributing to community.

Personal Agency: Becoming a Captain

A captain sets a path that she is certain of. A captain maintains her ship even if others jump off the ship. She doesn't spend a lot of time lamenting the fact that others are not on the ship. She continues on the journey, adjusting as necessary.

228

It is Bandura who details a framework for social agency. He describes agency as having four components: intentionality, forethought, self-reflectiveness, and self-reactiveness. Consider these explained in the context of the captain of a ship. Keep in mind that the captain always goes down with the ship. This is similar with you. You must stay. There is no sustainability in escaping your responsibilities and your role. You must deal with them as a captain steering a ship.

Intentionality in our captain analogy is setting a course with the expectation that this action increases the likelihood of arriving at a desired destination. The captain continues along the course, checking instruments, observing landmarks, and steering toward the port. If the captain finds herself off course, she double checks her activities to ascertain the irregularities that caused her to be off course.

For you, being an intentional captain means that you create principles that you can live with that support the change needed in yourself and in your environment. As you visualize the success that you desire, consider the moral and ethical guidelines that inform your actions and reactions. Establish these principles as your moral compass. Consider what indicators will signal that you are moving in the right direction including outcomes you can observe and impacts on people and your environment.

The challenge is not the decision. The challenge is living with the result of the decision whether good or bad, and having the courage to make as decisive a decision a second time. The opportunity is to evaluate all the possibilities prior to the decision, to learn from mistakes, but never question your responsibility to decide and continue forward to the next choice.

Forethought in our captain analogy is considering the weather and obstacles that may be faced along the planned route. The captain prepares with strategic hires and reserves of food and fuel. The captain's every action is guided by a consideration of what lies ahead. The best captains are not paralyzed by fear, but prepared for an extended journey and surprises.

For you, having forethought means investing in your vision of production. Reading and discussing how others have achieved, you can anticipate some of the challenges that lie ahead of you. Integrate the expenses of time, people, information and money into your plan. Perceive surprises as learning opportunities that increase your skill and assurance of success.

Our captain demonstrates **self-reactiveness** by responding to surprises or miscalculations with the same thoughtful approach that characterized the original planning. New information and challenges are a time to increase your awareness and recheck your plan. It may need to be changed, but any change is just as intentional and with the same approach to forethought as the original plan.

For you, self-reactiveness means defining your identity as a producer. The person that you are is uniquely capable of specific impact on the world. The validation of this fact comes from your interests, your personality, and even your frailties. Validation can also be derived from your experiences, both triumphs and setbacks. It was DeShazar who said, "There are no failures, only results." Integrate your results to continue your journey toward success.

Self-reflectiveness in our captain analogy is the ability of the captain to own the decisions she has made, and her ability to make the connection between the current course and those decisions. The captain can further evaluate new information and alternative choices to determine the next action.

For you, self-reflectiveness may be expressed in your review of relationships, knowledge, or roles that you undertake. Generally, it is the fruit of your production. Check its impact against your principles. If you are not reaching your potential or if you are creating consequences that you did not intend, investigate, articulate, and correct your behavior.

Creating a Movement

To apply your social role within society, you must conceptualize how to sustain your clarity while others conform steeped in deception, distraction, and disillusionment. They will be your detractors seeking to convince you to conform. Agency involves living a life that demonstrates the value and wisdom of intentionality, forethought, self-reflectiveness, and self-reactiveness. More than just a choice, and even beyond a consistent lifestyle, agency is a movement. It is a life that is intentionally contagious. Consistency results in the recruitment of likeminded others. The principles you identify and practice enable something bigger than you alone.

In order to activate this lifestyle of nonconformity as a movement, you will need to understand the anatomy of movements. Anatomy of a Movement is the operationalization of Bandura's Agentic Perspective. The movement is characterized by seven actions of social agency: investigate, educate, liberate, lead, act, create, and compete.

Investigate

Investigation describes your unique assessment of the mechanism employed in the conformity around you. That is, people in your social surroundings are comfortable with the status quo—the way things are. In order to address your delusion, you have to understand how it works for you. Conformity benefits you in some way. More than understanding the benefit, you must trace the mechanism of the benefit—how it works.

Investigation results in the celebration of principled growth and change, diversity, and informed decision making. As you understand the mechanisms of safety and predictability, you can surmise that conformity is not the only way to achieve them. Conformity works because it has a socially understood set of principles. The value is not in the conformity. The value is in the principles. People utilize principles to predict outcomes and maintain a sense of order and purpose. Such principles become the standards of conformity.

Conformity may suggest that diverse opinions cause chaos. Another view is that diverse opinions allow for alternative perspectives and may aid creativity. **Brainstorm opinions, perspectives, and starting points even if they seem far-fetched at first glance.** The consensus-seeking process of eliminating options will yield a set of choices that can be investigated further. This is more desirable than one, solitary option.

Time pressures seem to support conformity insisting that a decision be made quickly even if that means leaving the voices of others out of the consideration. Another view is that a decision resulting from the careful weighing of multiple options is an informed decision, more desirable than a quick decision. Organize your time in order to allow for a larger set of information in your decision making.

Educate

Education describes the intervention into the mechanism you observed during investigation. Your task is to reclaim the ownership of your ideas. With the ownership of ideas, you may begin to comprehend the role of producer. You may also begin to see the opportunity to integrate this social role into your interactions with others.

Education results in a new valuing of your ideas, definition of the producer role, and integration of the producer role into your social interactions. In short, **record your idea, establish your expertise and product, and engage your social role as producer.**

Write your ideas in a journal that you keep with you at all times. Your ideas are the single most unique expression of your humanness beyond the power of choice. The inspiration, whenever it comes, should be more fully respected through your action of writing it down. This respectful action allows you to build on your thoughts over time. As you grow in access to the means of production, you are able to put your ideas into practice providing a new opportunity for engagement and learning.

Identify your expertise and your product. Your expertise is a competence that you bring to every interaction. It supports your social role by both communicating its message and inspiring others to share their gift. Feed your expertise with knowledge from multiple, even competing sources. Ask yourself the tough questions, and seek answers, even answers that seem contradictory. Your work at synthesis of the antithetical concepts will advance your competence.

Engage relationships that support your producer role. This means both the finding of supportive relationships and locating the need for your competence. Through practice and educating others, you find and refine your voice. In their questions and point of view, you find the elements of wisdom that you have since considered basic. You find the beauty in the lessons you take for granted. In education, you find the highest calling of the producer—to provide a foundation of knowledge and experience for the next generation.

Liberate

Liberation describes effort to address the automatic behaviors that support conformity. The comfortable relationship between your conformity and benefit must be broken by revealing the comparative detriment you experience through conformity. That is, liberation is the revelation that you are not better off leaving well enough alone. A need for progress necessitates a search for excellence. In the search for excellence, you benefit yourself and others.

The further revelation of liberation is that others are not your obstacle. You are the obstacle to your success. Your labor is not your greatest contribution. Your ideas are your greatest contribution. The goal and motivation is not money. The goal is social capital that accesses the means of production. **Cultivate value through production. Redefine labor and leisure. Seek social capital.**

Outline the potential benefit of producing your ideas. Once you see the value of your unique contribution as it is produced (or as it has the potential to be produced), you realize the detriment of conformity. The challenges remain as obstacles until an individual decides to go against convention or to supplement convention in order to try something new. You are better able to see this potential in others when you recognize it within yourself.

Redefine labor as different from production. Conceptualize your contribution as more than just what you can DO. Your mind, your imagination, your desire for another way are all components required in a new and inventive solution. Your task is not to work harder. You are to work smarter. This does not dispense with labor, but it is an understanding of labor as only one component. You are not done once you have labored. You must nurture, disseminate, and revise.

Define social capital as a primary mechanism to access resources. Simply stated, you do not have to do it all yourself. More honestly, it would take you much too long to do it yourself. The network, the finances, the information, and the time needed would be outside of your reach even with two lifetimes. You must seek out those who understand legacy and generativity. They will give of their network, finances, information, and time to promote your ideas. They only ask that you allow them to help. They require that you value their contribution by producing.

Lead

Leadership describes both quality and activity. The quality is above reproach, self-vetted, and transparent. The activity is to set the agenda in written form, clear with action steps and indicators for independent evaluation. Leadership results in a strategic plan including explicit opportunities for newcomers to engage in the movement based on their desires AND expertise. Willing workers who do not arrive with identified or compatible expertise are educated into areas of the movement that best utilize their skills or areas that build on transferrable skills. Another alternative for non-compatible expertise is to expand the movement to accommodate a new area. Creation of a parallel or supportive movement is yet another option. Leadership must **communicate vision, outline principles, and establish the indicators of success**.

Articulate a vision complete with actions steps. Vision work begins to call teams to collective action. The collaboration and single-mindedness toward a goal can look like the conformity that the anatomy of a movement called you out of. Yet, this vision has two components that are beyond the status quo. First, this vision of a movement values the diversity of the participants recognizing that it is that difference that spurs the movement. Second, this vision celebrates the creation of off-shoot movements who continue the branching and the increase in territory.

Outline criteria for collaboration. The principals of the movement must be expressed in a code of ethical conduct providing explanations of the responsibility, roles, knowledge, and mechanisms of the movement. These components are open system and reviewed every 3 to 5 years allowing for creative destruction—a movement to create a new movement beyond the current one.

Articulate the impact you want to have. The intentions must be clear from the individual, to the group, to the collective, to the community. The indicators of progress must be monitored through a formative and summative feedback loop. Progress, failure, updates, tweaks, and overhauls are a collective undertaking. These fixes are to be transparent, archived, and digitally searchable.

Act

Action describes an obvious step of implementation. It also describes a systematic approach to the operations of the movement. What many do not account for is the marketing and messaging, the education, and the convening that is required in any collaboration. As the initiatives add new areas of focus, expand their scope, and extend across time, these considerations become even more critical to success. Action will **communicate the set of principles on a schedule of training and a schedule of conferencing**.

Create a schedule of training that responds to the information and lifestyle needs of the collective members. Produce the training with competency-based education methods to ensure mastery, application, and internalization through critical discussion. Ensure that the training system is consistent with the principles of the movement. Support collective action, self-reflection, and competence as well as individualization, alternate points of view, and discussion.

Create a schedule for periodic reflection and discussion with supportive others. This is the federation model. Rather than a centralized system of command and control, create a system of centralized resource sharing including money, information, and personnel. Make these resources available through a digital portal for access at any time, from any interface.

Create

Creativity describes the reality that effective leadership and action will result in former volunteers, line workers, and interested learners who become regional directors, non-profit founders, and social entrepreneurs. The movement must be responsible for the development of these new institutions as well as the leaders themselves. Leadership and action provided the model and the education. Creativity must provide the operational knowledge and evaluative structure for the newly created institutions.

Consider creativity as a three part initiation of the institution. First, reflect on the history and the model of other institutions seeking justice, progress, and altruism. Second, capture in writing that history as instruction on best practices and opportunities for improvement as the new initiative is launched. Third, ensure that the new initiative spawns other initiatives and does not consider itself the end all. In short, **reflect on the history of the movement. Capture that history. Seed new movements**.

Define creativity as form and art, valuing both rules and freedom. Beyond the dualistic view of human life, reflect on the ability of both order and chaos to coexist in the movement. Maintain a log that catalogs the operations and indicators of this grand experiment. Emphasize that singularly unique reality of the movement. To take its place of respect, every movement must spawn other movements.

Compete

Invest in positive competition rather than negative competition. A depth of opportunity is represented by friend and foe alike. No matter the proposed relationship, know that you can utilize energy for your motivation. You can gain even from the success of others. And when you collaborate, you can reach beyond your imagination.

Your challenge is to compete. It is not self-conceit, but positive competition. Review your entertainment. Determine whether it is productive recreation or self-medication. As you gain the knowledge that you desire, contribute your best. Grow even greater contributions for the future.

You have not accomplished anything on your own. You may not have appreciated the person, the advice they gave, or the example they demonstrated. But, to your credit, you learned the lesson that was available to you. To realize the value of that lesson, you must realize the value of that person. It is not a call to reunite with those who have hurt you. It is an example of the potential for those who support you to provide both lesson and encouragement beyond what you can think or ask. If even your interactions with your enemies can be used as lessons for you, how much more will your interactions with your friends be valued?

This reveals a useful insight into competition. Realize that the value of others to you is the challenge they bring to you. Once you accept this, you begin to benefit from the motivation you feel watching others do their best. You gain strength even in the midst of competition. You find curiosity even in the face of authority telling you no. This is positive competition.

The greatest experience of competition is modeled in our relationship. Limiting challenge, limits creativity. Though I am interested in assisting you, I will not allow your sluggishness to impede my progress. I will produce while inviting you to participate. I will organize a place for you in the midst of my production cycle, but your choices will not derail my production.

When we talk, our discussions will include information on your ideas and next steps. I will share my latest products and achievements. My interest in you is spurred by my attempts to find connections between your ideas and my needs for production. When I find a match, I will invite you into collaboration. I will challenge you to produce.